PRESENTING BUFFALO BILL

THE MAN WHO INVENTED THE WILD WEST

CANDACE FLEMING

A NEAL PORTER BOOK
ROARING BROOK PRESS
NEW YORK

Text copyright © 2016 by Candace Fleming
A Neal Porter Book
Published by Roaring Brook Press
Roaring Brook Press is a division of
Holtzbrinck Publishing Holdings Limited Partnership
175 Fifth Avenue, New York, New York 10010
mackids.com
First published in the United States of America in 2016 by Roaring Brook Press

Library of Congress Cataloging-in-Publication Data

Fleming, Candace, author.
    Presenting Buffalo Bill : the man who invented the Wild West / Candace
Fleming.—First edition.
        pages cm
    "A Neal Porter Book."
    Includes bibliographical references.
    Audience: Ages 10–14.
    ISBN 978-1-59643-763-0 (hardcover)
    ISBN 978-1-59643-747-2 (e-book)
    1. Buffalo Bill, 1846–1917—Juvenile literature.   2. Pioneers—West
(U.S.)—Biography—Juvenile literature.   3. Entertainers—United States—
Biography—Juvenile literature.   4. Buffalo Bill's Wild West Show—History—
Juvenile literature.   5. West (U.S.)—Biography—Juvenile literature.   I. Title.

F594.F63 2016
978'.02092—dc23
                                                              2015035540

Our books may be purchased in bulk for promotional, educational, or
business use. Please contact your local bookseller or the Macmillan
Corporate and Premium Sales Department at (800) 221-7945 ext. 5442
or by e-mail at MacmillanSpecialMarkets@macmillan.com.

First edition 2016
Book design by Roberta Pressel
Printed in the United States of America by R. R. Donnelley & Sons Company,
Harrisonburg, Virginia

10   9   8   7   6   5   4   3   2   1

To Mr. P., with love

CONTENTS

A NOTE FROM THE AUTHOR

You will notice that throughout this book I have—whenever possible—identified American Indian people as members of specific tribes. This is the preferred usage. Still, I have also used the phrases *Native American*, *American Indian*, *Native*, and *Native performer* to refer more broadly to peoples indigenous to North America. Additionally, I have used *Indian* when it appears in historical material from which I am quoting or when it is used in an established term such as *Bureau of Indian Affairs* or *Indian Agent*. I realize all these terms are problematic, and have been much debated. But terminology is needed. Always my intention when referring to people outside my own cultural heritage is to be respectful and accurate.

"Buffalo Bill" Cody in 1895 at the pinnacle of his Wild West career.

INTRODUCTION

When I was a kid in the 1960s, westerns like *Gunsmoke* and *Bonanza* were the biggest hits on prime-time television. Every week these shows broadcast an idea of the Wild West into millions of American homes. Stampeding buffalo and runaway stagecoaches. Shoot-outs and show-downs. Wide-open spaces and the call of the cavalry's bugle. I thrilled to it all. But by far the most appealing image was that of the rugged cowboy. In episode after episode—using nothing but his superior roping, shooting, and riding skills—he faced down vicious outlaws and fierce American Indians. Even then, I understood he was more than a tele-vision hero. He was supposed to be representing America itself—courageous and freedom-loving; a shining symbol of our nation's conquest of the West. He was a legend, a tall tale, a myth.

Every human group creates myths—those fables and fantasies that help people make sense of their history. And in the United States, the winning of the West is the most popular myth. As it's often told, Euro-peans sailed across the ocean to a primitive continent. Surviving brutal conditions, they labored to conquer the land. Once settled in the East, they bravely turned their faces westward. Courageous and indepen-dent, they fought American Indians. They built farms and towns and democratic societies. They spread civilization from sea to shining sea. It's a stirring story.

Too bad it's not accurate.

That's the problem with myths: they're not overly concerned with facts. Yes, taming the Wild West is a fundamental part of how we built our nation. It is a pivotal part of the American story. But real western history is not so romantic. It is messy, sometimes grim, and anything but simple.

So where did this mythology come from?

Certainly, TV westerns perpetuated it. So did Hollywood filmmakers and cowboy stars like John Wayne. But who came before that? Where did it all start?

With a hardscrabble frontiersman who became America's legendary showman: William Frederick "Buffalo Bill" Cody.

An iconic image of Buffalo Bill, rifle in hand and riding a big white horse (c. 1900).

FANFARE

Outside the London arena, William F. Cody sat astride his favorite stallion, Charlie, and inspected his show's performers. He had brought his entire outfit—218 performers, 180 horses, 18 buffalo, 10 elk, 5 wild Texas steers, 4 donkeys, 2 deer, and 2 bears, not to mention a stagecoach, a replica log cabin, canvas scenery, wagons, 36 brass instruments, rifles, saddles, and more bullets than a man could count—all the way from America. He'd come with hopes of striking it rich, of selling millions of tickets and making millions of dollars. But never in his wildest dreams had he expected this—a command performance ordered by Queen Victoria of England herself!

Cody had come a long way from herding cows at five dollars a week to performing for royalty. As he watched his troupe gather, his mind must have flashed back to the sad boy who'd been forced to go to work full-time after his father's death. Cody claimed that between his eleventh birthday and fifteenth birthday, he freighted wagons across the frontier, survived a starvation winter at Fort Bridger, skirmished with some American Indians and made friends with others, rode the Pony Express, prospected for gold in Colorado, and hunted buffalo on the Great Plains. And he wove all these adventures into his show. Giving them titles like "Attack on the Settler's Cabin," "Buffalo Hunt as It Was in the Far West," and "Cowboy Fun," Cody reenacted the experiences of his young life for the entertainment of his audiences.

And tonight, his audience was the Queen of England herself!

His dark brown eyes swept over his troupers. All looked in order. There stood Annie Oakley, "Little Sure Shot," her rifle slung over her buckskin-clad shoulder. Behind her, bushy-bearded John Nelson perched atop the old Deadwood stagecoach—the one Cody had won in a coin toss—reins in his hands and ready to go. The showman looked for Lillian Smith. Lillian was good with a gun, too. But the flighty fifteen-year-old sometimes arrived late for performances. Not today, though. There she stood along with champion roper Jim "Kid" Willoughby and "Broncho Charlie" Miller, dressed to the nines and raring to go. Behind them, already mounted on horseback, waited Buck Taylor, "King of the Cowboys," along with his fellow riders. Those boys could ride anything they could get a leg across—bulls, buffalo, horses. And the horses were real buckers. "There's nothing fake in my whole show," Cody liked to say. There were more than ninety Lakota men, women, and children, too. Wearing buckskin and feathers, a group of warriors sat bareback on their ponies, waiting.

Inside the arena, the Cowboy Band struck up a lively tune. It was time for the grand entrance. Shouting, the Lakota warriors galloped into the arena at breakneck speed, the pounding of their horses' hooves echoing across the wide-open space. Right behind them, six-shooters blazing, plunged the cowboys, followed by Mexican vaqueros, grizzled frontiersmen, rifle-toting Texas rangers, and detachments dressed as the U.S. cavalry and artillery wildly waving the Stars and Stripes. Around and around the arena the performers looped until finally they formed a colorful square. Falling suddenly silent, they turned and faced the queen.

There was a suspense-filled pause.

Then a trumpet sounded.

And in rode Cody. Wheeling his prancing horse before the queen, he came to a quick stop. Charlie reared, standing on his hind legs.

In her seat, Queen Victoria politely clapped her lace-gloved hands.

Letting the horse down, Cody swept off his big sombrero. The long brown hair that he'd rolled up under it fell down around his shoulders.

Now, head held high, Cody prepared to send his deep voice soaring over the grandstand. And even though the only people in the grandstand today were the queen, her military escort, and an entourage of aristocrats, he shouted:

"Welcome, your Majesty, to the Wild West!"

Reenactment of the "Attack on the Settler's Cabin" (c. 1894). Buffalo Bill (far right and with his back to the camera) and a band of cowboys, scouts, and frontiersmen come to the rescue.

ACT ONE

The Boy Will Cody
Or
"Attack on the Settler's Cabin by Indians and Rescue by Buffalo Bill with His Scouts, Cowboys, and Mexicans."

—Buffalo Bill's Wild West Program, 1894

A Scene from the Wild West

The audience leans forward. In the center of the arena sits a log cabin. Behind it, painted scenery depicts thick woods, peaceful green meadows, and sparkling streams. Into this blissful setting steps the weary hunter, rifle slung over his shoulder. His son waves happily to him from the cabin window. His wife, with open arms, welcomes him at the door. The hunter is home at last.

There comes a shout. It is a Lakota warrior in paint and feathers. He charges toward the cabin.

Pushing his wife behind him, the hunter aims his rifle. He fires.

The attacker drops to the showground. Lifeless.

Now dozens of screaming Lakota—some on foot, some on horseback—hurtle into the scene. They surge toward the cabin.

The hunter and his wife barricade themselves inside. Loading and reloading their weapons they all—even the boy—fire at their attackers.

The arena fills with gun smoke. Audience members' ears ring from the rifle shots and war cries.

Inside the cabin, the hunter and his family are tiring. They are almost out of bullets. All appears lost.

And then another shout!

Riding into the fray, guns blazing, is Buffalo Bill. Behind him gallops a posse of rifle-toting cowboys. There are more gunshots, more bodies dropping to the ground. At last, defeated, the Lakota leap onto their horses and gallop away.

The grateful hunter and his family step out of their cabin. They thank Buffalo Bill and his cowboys. As they do, the audience leaps to its feet, clapping and whistling and tossing hats in the air.

A nugget of truth lay behind this popular act from the Wild West show. William Cody *had* faced savage foes. He was just ten years old when he first pointed a rifle at a man. Less than a year later, he outran a gang of would-be assassins. But in real life, it wasn't American Indians who'd threatened and terrified little Will Cody. Instead, it was his fellow frontier settlers who attacked his home.

But not at first.

At first, remembered his sister Helen, there was "dancing sunshine . . . wood and meadow." And the birth of a baby boy.

THE FORTUNE-TELLER MAKES A PREDICTION

According to family legend, Isaac and Mary Cody believed the birth of their second son, William Frederick, on February 26, 1846, fulfilled a mystical prophecy. Seven years earlier, when she was still unmarried, Mary had been visiting her sister in Louisville, Kentucky, when a traveling fortune-teller arrived in town. On a lark, the sisters decided to go. They stepped into the darkened parlor with its mysterious cards and crystal ball.

The fortune-teller took Mary's hand in her own. Turning it palm-side up, she studied the lines she found there, tracing them with her finger. Then she shuffled her cards. "You will meet your future husband on the steamboat by which you are expected to return home," the fortune-teller finally said. "[You] will be married to him within a year and bear him three sons, of whom only the second [will] live, but the name of this son [will] be known all over the world."

Mary did not believe a word of it. That is, not until the first part of the fortune-teller's words came true. She *did* meet Isaac on the steamboat home, and she *did* marry him within a year. So when she gave birth to her second son in the Codys' four-bedroom cabin just west of Le Claire, Iowa, a town on a bend of the Mississippi River, both parents looked on him with special hope.

Will grew into a smart, lovable boy who was doted on by his older siblings—Martha, Samuel, and Julia—and later worshipped by the younger ones—Eliza, Helen, May, and Charlie. "He was a superior being," his sister Helen once admitted. "Never did we weaken in our belief that great things were in store for our brother."

The only known photograph of Will's mother, Mary Ann Cody, taken around 1860.

His mother, too, fussed over him. She never punished him and only rarely scolded him. Mostly, she worried. Will, it was plain to see, had been born with an adventurous spirit that led him into all kinds of mischief and even danger.

He exhibited this spirit early on. One day in the summer of 1847, when Will was a year old, the town doctor stopped in at the Codys' for a visit. After tying up his horse—"a mean horse [that liked] to kick"—he went inside. Little Will seized his chance. As his family busied itself with its company, Will toddled out the door. He made straight for the cantankerous animal. He was already standing behind the horse's hind legs, his pudgy arms stretching up to pat the horse's flank, when his older sister Julia saw him. Racing outside, the four-year-old girl snatched up her brother just as the horse snorted and kicked. Its powerful hooves just missed the children. "They all sayed I saved Will's life," Julia later recalled, "[and] when the doctor came out . . . he called me a brave little girl."

It was obvious that Will needed to be watched every minute. But how? Isaac had a farm to run—cows to milk and fields to plow. And Mary was busy morning to night hoeing the garden, shelling beans, fetching water from the spring, making soap, knitting socks, and cooking. So she turned to Julia. "Your charge is to look after Willie," Mary told the girl. And although Julia was just four years old at the time, she took the job seriously. She never left the boy unattended, not even when she went to school.

The next fall, Julia, along with Martha and Samuel, trudged through woods and meadow to a one-room schoolhouse built of logs. Here Miss Helen Goodrige taught the basics of reading and arithmetic to a handful of students ranging in age from five to fourteen. Eighteen-month-old Will went along, too. But the lively toddler was disruptive. He ran around the room, dipping his fingers

Is this really a photograph of four-year-old Will Cody? The picture was found in the Cody Bible, and the inscription on its back identifies it as such. Still, scholars who recently examined it are doubtful.

into ink bottles and drawing on walls and furniture. Recalled Julia, "[I] took him outdoors when he wanted to go, and when he got sleepy [I] just laid him on one of the benches." Neither Julia nor Will learned much that year.

SKINNY-DIPPING, SKIFFS, AND SKIPPING SCHOOL

In 1849, news that gold had been discovered in California reached the Cody farm. Overnight, Isaac was seized with gold fever. All he could think about, according to Will, was "that exciting climate of gold, flowers, oranges, sweet odors and fighting whiskey." Selling his property, he bought a covered wagon and prepared to move his family across the country.

The trip, however, didn't happen. "Why, I never knew," wrote Will years later. Some claimed it was because Isaac fell ill. Others say it was because the group he planned to travel with got cold feet after hearing reports about American Indian attacks on the trail. Either way, the Codys remained in Iowa. Renting a house in downtown Le Claire, Isaac went to work as a stage driver on the route between Davenport and Chicago.

Will became a town boy. Barefoot, wearing a brimless hat, one suspender, and a mischievous smile, he raided his neighbors' melon patches, rode other people's horses when he could catch them on the town square, and tied his friends' clothing to the tops of trees while they were skinny-dipping in the river. "I was quite as bad," Will later confessed, "though no worse, than the ordinary, every-day boy."

In 1851, Will—now five years old—was sent to school again. For the next year he struggled with his numbers and letters. "By diligence . . . I managed to familiarize myself with the alphabet, but further progress was arrested by a suddenly developed love of skiff-riding on the Mississippi," he later admitted.

Day after day, Will and a handful of friends would sneak away from the schoolhouse. Heading down to the river, they would "borrow" one of the many small flat-bottomed boats that lined the bank. After rowing into the water, they would float along with the current, their fishing lines dragging behind them. Indeed, skiff-riding "occupied so much of my time thereafter that really I found no convenient opportunity for further attendance at school," said Will. His parents, he claimed, never knew he was skipping class. How he managed to escape Julia's ever-watchful eye, however, remains a mystery.

Then one morning Will and two other boys were out on the river when they suddenly found themselves far from the shore. Spring rains had swollen the Mississippi, creating a roiling current filled with tree branches and green ribbons of vegetation. The little boat bumped and rocked. "We lost our presence of mind, as well as our oars," recalled Will. Terrified, the boys screamed for help. Minutes later, a man in a canoe came to their rescue and towed them to shore. But the boys' troubles did not stop there. "We had stolen the boat . . . We each received a . . . whipping." It was the end of Will's skiff-riding days.

The same year, the mischievous boy took his mother's keepsake five-franc silver coin (similar to a silver dollar) from her sewing basket. Strolling down to the riverbank where a group of older boys were playing, he showed them the coin. Then he walked innocently out onto the pier.

The boys returned to their play.

But just minutes later, Will frantically began searching his pockets. "I guess it must have dropped in the river," he exclaimed.

He had the boys' instant attention. "What dropped?" they asked.

"That five-franc piece," he replied. "Let's see if you can find it."

So while the five-year-old stood on the pier and gave directions, the older boys waded and groped in the shallow water, searching with fingers and toes for the coin.

Meanwhile, someone ran to tell Mary Cody what had happened. Furious, she stormed down to the river, switch in hand, and shouted, "Willie! I told you not to take that [coin] didn't I? And now you've gone and lost it in the river. Come here! I want to see you."

"Aw, Ma," replied Will. "I ain't lost it. Here it is. I was just learnin' 'em how to dig for gold in California." And he handed over the coin, safe and dry.

Already, Will was exhibiting a talent for leadership.

In 1852, Isaac uprooted his family again. This time he moved them to a large farm in Walnut Grove, fifteen miles west of Le Claire. For the next year the family lived in a pleasant, roomy farmhouse set in the sunlight against a background of cool green wood and mottled meadow. Will roamed the countryside, his big black dog, Turk, padding along behind. He built quail traps with string, twigs, and boxes, and checked them twice a day. "I greatly enjoyed studying the habits of the little birds, and devising [ways] to take them in," Will recalled. "Thus I think it was that I acquired my love for hunting."

A DARK AND MOURNFUL DAY

On a September afternoon in 1853, the Codys gathered around the table for the midday meal. The family had grown, and now seven children tucked into Mary's corn dodgers and crispy fried pork: eighteen-year-old Martha, twelve-year-old Samuel, ten-year-old Julia, seven-year-old Will, five-year-old Eliza, three-year-old Helen, and Mary (called May), who was not quite one. Meal finished, Samuel pushed back from the table. It was time to bring the cows in from the pasture two miles away.

Eager for any chance to sit a horse, Will offered to help. And Samuel agreed. He must have been glad of the extra hands since Isaac

13

wouldn't be helping. Their father was headed to a political meeting at Sherman's Tavern, about a mile away.

The boys went down to the barn. Will clambered bareback onto a slow old mare. Even though he'd been riding since he was old enough to straddle a saddle, his parents refused to let him ride anything but the gentlest horse.

Samuel, though, saddled up Betsy Baker. Betsy came from racing stock, and she was nervous. Time and again their mother had told him not to ride Betsy. The horse was too unpredictable and sometimes behaved badly. But Samuel liked her because she was so fast.

Out of the barnyard the boys rode, Betsy skimming over the fields like a bird, Will's horse lumbering behind. The riders turned onto the road where the schoolhouse sat. Its doors opened, and the students spilled out.

How could Samuel resist such an audience? He *had* to show off his horsemanship skills. He pulled back on the reins.

Betsy Baker's temper flared. Rearing onto her hind legs, she furiously struck the air with her front hooves before plunging forward to kick out her back legs.

Samuel clung to the reins and kept to the saddle as Betsy reared and bucked again and again.

Then suddenly she calmed, seemingly giving up the fight.

Aware of the schoolchildren's wide eyes looking at him, Samuel cried victoriously, "Ah, Betsy Baker, you didn't quite come it that time!"

At that, the mare reared up, up, up.

Samuel clung to the horse as she hurtled over backward, crushing the boy beneath her.

Will arrived just as Betsy Baker scrambled to her feet.

Samuel, though, remained on the ground. He didn't move.

As the schoolmaster and a group of older students carried the unconscious boy to a nearby house, Will slammed his heels into the sides of his horse. He had to fetch Isaac.

Sherman's Tavern must have seemed a thousand miles away. Arriving at last, he told his father the news. Frantic, Isaac pulled Will off the mare, leaped up in his place, and galloped off for the schoolhouse. Will was left to drive his father's ox-drawn wagon back by himself.

When he finally arrived at the house where Samuel had been taken, he found his entire family huddled around his brother's bedside, weeping bitterly. The boy's injuries were fatal, the doctor told them. There was nothing to be done. "He died the next morning," Will remembered.

THE CODYS HEAD WEST

After Samuel's death, life became almost unbearable for Isaac and Mary. Everywhere they looked they saw their older boy—in the barn, in the pasture, at the supper table. "Gloom fell over the farm," remembered Will. "Father . . . [was] heartbroken over it."

It was time to leave. Isaac, who had not been content with Iowa since his failed plans to move to California, now set his sights on Kansas.

In early 1854, the U.S. Senate passed a bill opening up the territories of Nebraska and Kansas to settlement. All a man had to do to acquire territorial land from the government was file a claim and "make improvements," that is, build a house and grow crops.

"Now is the time to make claims," urged one Missouri newspaper. "The country is swarming with [settlers]. Men on horseback, with cup and skillet, ham, flour and coffee tied behind them, and axe on shoulder, are hurrying westward, companies with flags flying are staking out the prairies, trees are falling, tents are stretching, cabins are going up . . . Hurrah for Kansas!"

Isaac sold the farm and all the stock except for enough mules and horses to pull his three wagons. He loaded up the family's furniture, as well as the farm equipment. And he hired a man to help drive the rigs to the new territory. Then on a bright spring morning in April 1854, he gave the wagon reins a slap. The Codys headed west.

The journey took weeks. They traveled across Iowa, and through a small section of Missouri. Since this region was already settled, there was no reason to camp or hunt. Instead, the family stopped each night "at the best hotels," recalled Julia, where the maids helped put the children to bed. At last, after crossing the Missouri River by ferry, the family arrived in the new territory.

Eastern Kansas seemed to promise a bright future. From the top of Salt Creek Hill the family looked down on a valley—"the most beautiful valley I [had] ever seen," recalled Will.

But it wasn't the grassy hills or sparkling streams that dazzled the eight-year-old boy. It was the sight of a long line of prairie schooners moving through the valley. Will "got wild with excitement," remembered Julia. Echoing through the valley came the clink and rattle of the wagons, the sharp snap of bullwhips, and the lowing of cattle.

"Where [are] they going?" Will asked his father.

"Utah and California," replied Isaac.

"Oh, my," the boy reportedly gushed, "that is what I am going to do [someday]."

Wasting little time, Isaac staked his claim in Salt Creek Valley. He planted a spring crop of hay. And he hired men to help build a two-story, seven-room log house. While the family waited for it to be completed, they lived in tents on their new land—"the first time I ever camped, or slept upon the ground," recalled Will.

FLYING OVER THE PRAIRIE
ON A PONY NAMED PRINCE

The Salt Creek Trail ran past the Codys' Kansas homestead, and there was always something interesting to see. Sometimes the children in the westbound wagons waved to Will as they passed. Cavalrymen from nearby Fort Leavenworth often stopped in. Prospectors, scouts, guides, and traders dropped in with tales of the far west.

But to Will's mind, the most fascinating visitors were members of the Kickapoo tribe. They came often to the Cody place to trade venison for colored beads or to trade animal pelts for blankets, knives, or kettles. Sometimes they brought along their children, and Will made friends with some of the boys. He tried to learn their language, although he later admitted that his "conversations were very limited." He did better at learning their games. And he admired their ponies. Hard-fleshed and trim-legged, the ponies had delicately curved necks and small bodies, making them fast and powerful. Will longed to own one himself. When would his father ever let him ride anything but the family's old mare?

One morning a band of Kickapoo arrived at the Codys'. To Will's surprise, his father began trading for *two* ponies. The first, a gentle bay mare, was meant for Julia. Will named the horse Dolly. The second, a spirited stallion, was Will's. "I called him Prince," he said.

A real eye-catcher, Prince was a copper shade of chestnut with a lighter mane and tail. Will couldn't wait to hop onto his back and tear across the fields. Problem was, Prince had never been ridden. When Will patted the pony's withers, he snorted and jumped away. "I was somewhat disappointed at this," confessed Will.

As luck would have it, just hours later a rider came over the green crest of the valley. Trotting onto the Codys' land, he hopped off his horse and made his introductions. His name, he said, was Horace

Billings, and he was camped nearby with a group of Californians bringing back a herd of mustangs to market.

Will had never met anyone like Horace Billings. He was a "genuine Western man . . . dressed in a complete suit of buckskin, beautifully trimmed and beaded."

After a few minutes of conversation, Horace turned to the boy. "Little one," Horace said, "I see you are working with your pony. [He] is wild yet."

"Yes," answered Will. "[He] . . . has never been ridden."

"Well, I'll ride him for you," cried Horace. "Come on."

Quick as a wink, Horace untied Prince's rope and, making a half loop around the pony's nose, jumped onto his back.

"In a moment he was flying over the prairie," remembered Will, "the untamed steed rearing and pitching . . . But the man was not unseated." Obviously, Horace was an experienced horseman. "I watched his every movement," said Will.

Horace stayed on the pony until it calmed. Then trotting over to Will, he hopped off and tossed the boy the rope. "Here's your pony," he said. "He's all right now."

But Horace wasn't done showing off yet. Untying Isaac's horse, Little Gray, from a nearby tree, the Californian demonstrated a few riding tricks. Galloping full tilt across the prairie, he stood straight up on Little Gray's back. As he passed Will and his father, Horace jumped to the ground. Then letting the horse have the full length of rope, he gave a mighty tug. Incredibly, the animal did a complete somersault.

Will thought this was "really wonderful . . . skillful and daring."

"Oh, that's nothing," said Horace. "I was raised on horseback." And he told the Codys about his life traveling with a circus and becoming a celebrated bareback rider. And as the conversation wore on, the three discovered an incredible coincidence. Horace was Isaac's nephew—the long-lost son of his sister Sophia!

Horace decided to move in with his uncle Isaac. For the rest of the summer, he worked on the Cody homestead, cutting logs and building split-rail fences. In his spare time, he showed Will how to train his pony. Soon Prince came when Will whistled and kneeled down so the boy could climb easily onto his back.

But Horace became bored with farmwork, so he took a job rounding up the wild horses that still stampeded across the Kansas prairie. Sometimes he took Will along. Because the horses had to be caught with a lasso, Horace taught the boy how to throw one. He also taught him how to throw an obstinate horse to the ground. "Everything that he did, I wanted to do," said Will. "He was a hero in my eyes and I wished to follow in his footsteps."

Sadly, Horace did not stay on with the Codys. In the spring of 1855, longing for the adventure of the far west, he signed up with a wagon train headed for Utah. By that time, bragged Will, "I had become a remarkably good rider for a youth."

The family never heard from Horace again.

BLEEDING KANSAS

When Congress had opened up the Kansas Territory to settlers, it had dodged the most controversial subject in America—slavery. Should slaves be allowed in Kansas or not? Congress chose not to answer this question. Instead, it decided to allow the people of the territory to decide for themselves. This decision unleashed, as one U.S. senator called it, "a hell of a storm."

In the North, abolitionist groups formed organizations that sent thousands of antislavery settlers, called "free-soilers," into the territory. "Kansas is the great battlefield where a mighty conflict is to be waged against the monster slavery," wrote Julia Lovejoy, a settler from New Hampshire, "and [it] will be routed and slain. Amen and Amen." The Lovejoys, like so many others, were willing to give up their old lives to keep the soil of Kansas free from slavery. They were also prepared to fight if necessary. "I can assure you, every man . . . was prepared for them," said Mrs. Lovejoy.

Meanwhile, the South responded by sending thousands of armed men, mostly from Missouri, across the border. Called "border ruffians," these men promised to defend the institution of slavery "with the bayonet and with blood" and "to kill every damned abolitionist in the district."

There was little local government to speak of. "Govern Kansas?" said Wilson Shannon, the second territorial governor. "You might as well have attempted to govern hell."

Violence became inevitable. Every day brought kidnappings and killings. People were tarred and feathered, their homes burned, their property stolen.

"We are in the midst of . . . a war of extermination," wrote Julia Lovejoy. "Freedom and slavery are interlocked in deadly embrace, and death is certain for one or the other party."

Seemingly overnight, the Codys found themselves living in one of the most dangerous places in America—what some people were calling Bleeding Kansas. Still, Isaac wasn't worried about getting mixed up in the turmoil. He'd come to Kansas to make money, and nothing else. Besides, he wasn't an abolitionist. He was all for letting slave owners keep their slaves, just not in Kansas. Like many settlers, Isaac resented the possibility of competing against black labor. For this reason, he believed Kansas should be an all-white territory, a place where black people—free or slave—were outlawed.

A Speech and a Stabbing

On September 18, 1854, Isaac headed home from Fort Leavenworth. He must have been feeling pleased with himself. He'd just struck a deal with the fort commander to provide hay for the army's horses—hay that already stood cut and stacked in his fields.

As he turned onto the Salt Creek Trail, he noticed a large group of men in front of Rively's trading post. This wasn't unusual. On most Saturday nights, men gathered there to drink whiskey and talk politics. Isaac knew this part of the territory was filled with pro-slavery men, so he figured the people in the crowd were mostly cursing and railing against abolitionists.

He didn't intend to stop. But as he passed by, some of the men called out to him. They grabbed the reins of his horse, insisting he say a few words on the issue of slavery.

Isaac tried to beg off. It was late. He was tired. His family was waiting.

But the men would not take no for an answer. "Speech! Speech!" they shouted. Pulling him from the saddle, they hustled him over to a large, wooden dry goods crate being used as a stage. Hop up there, they insisted. Give us a speech.

Isaac gave in. "Gentlemen, . . . [Kansas] should be a *white* State," he began, ". . . that [blacks], whether free or slave, should never be allowed to locate within its limits."

His words shocked the crowd. They knew Isaac's brother Elijah was a slave owner in Missouri and had assumed Isaac and Elijah held the same political views. They began hissing and booing.

"Get down from that box!" one man hollered.

"You black abolitionist, shut up!" cried another.

"Kill him!" called yet another.

Isaac tried to explain he wasn't an abolitionist. "I believe in letting

This woodcut from Cody's 1879 autobiography shows the stabbing of his father, a life-altering event for the eight-year-old boy. Sadly, no photographs of Isaac Cody exist.

slavery remain as it now exists," he shouted above the noise. "These are my sentiments, gentlemen, and let me tell you—"

He never finished his sentence. A drunken, swearing man named Charles Dunn pushed his way through the angry mob. Pulling out a huge bowie knife, Dunn leaped onto the crate and stabbed Isaac twice.

Isaac reeled and fell to the ground.

Dunn sprang after him. Aiming for Isaac's heart, he raised his knife for one last thrust.

That's when M. Pierce Rively, owner of the trading post, stepped in. Grabbing Dunn's wrist, he dragged the would-be killer away.

Rively's actions sobered the crowd. No one argued when Dr. Hathaway, who was also attending the gathering, took Isaac into the store and examined his wounds. They were severe. His lung had been hit. Sending word to Mrs. Cody to bring a wagon, he suggested Isaac be taken to his brother's house in Missouri. Not only would he get better medical care there, but he'd be away from his angry neighbors. Let tempers cool, suggested the doctor. Mary Cody agreed.

For the next three weeks, Isaac recuperated at his brother's house. While he was gone, the anger of his pro-slavery neighbors continued to simmer. Ten days after the event, a local newspaper, the *Democratic Platform*, wrote about Isaac: "A Mr. Cody, a noisy abolitionist . . . was severely stabbed . . . but not enough to cause his death. The settlers on Salt Creek regret that his wound is not more dangerous."

DEATH THREATS, DISGUISES, AND DANGER

His father's speech, Will later said, "brought upon our family all of the misfortunes and difficulties which from that time on befell us." Within days of Isaac's return from Missouri, a "body of armed men mounted on horses rode up to our house and surrounded it."

Isaac, who was still bedridden, knew he was too weak to confront the men. His only hope, he realized, was escape. So he hastily disguised himself in his wife's clothing. Then, with the rim of Mary Cody's sunbonnet pulled low over his face, he boldly walked between the murderous horsemen and made his way out into the cornfield.

He hid there for three days, signaling to his family by raising the tip of his walking stick above the tall plants. After making sure all was clear, eight-year-old Will and eleven-year-old Julia plunged into the field carrying food, water, blankets, and clean bandages. "My first real work as a scout began then," Will later wrote, "for I had to keep constantly on watch for raids by [men] who had now sworn my father must die." Eventually, Isaac escaped to Fort Leavenworth, although exactly how he accomplished this is not known. He didn't dare return to his family for weeks.

Threats against Isaac were joined by attacks on his home and farm. Throughout that winter of 1854–55, pro-slavery neighbors drove off his horses and stole his livestock. Worst of all, they torched the hay he'd cut, stacked, and promised to Fort Leavenworth. Isaac wept. "In less than one hour the 3,000 [bale] of hay was in a blaze," remembered Julia. "All we could do was look at it."

Isaac, however, refused to be scared off; he continued improving his Salt Creek Valley home. In the spring of 1855, he built a barn for his new livestock and tried digging a well.

Around this time Mary started complaining about her children's lack of schooling. They hadn't stepped inside a classroom since they'd left Iowa a year earlier. So Isaac set up a school in a nearby abandoned cabin. After furnishing it with long benches and a blackboard, he hired a teacher, Miss Jennie Lyons. Soon twelve students—five of them Cody kids—bent over their slates. "It was a nice little school," recalled Julia.

Then one afternoon a gang of rifle-toting ruffians galloped up to the schoolhouse. Pushing open the door, they swaggered up to Miss Lyons's desk.

No "damned abolitionist," one of them told her, was going to be allowed to have a school.

"If [we have] to come back," threatened a second, "[we will] set fire to the schoolhouse and burn you all in it."

Added another nastily, "As Cody [has] the most brats in the school."

Terrified, Miss Lyons handed in her resignation that very afternoon.

The Cody children's schooling had lasted just three months.

"THE FIRST BLOOD [SHED]"

In the fall of 1855, a territory-wide election was held to choose representatives to Kansas's first legislature. On voting day, five thousand ruffians from Missouri flooded across the border. Seizing polling places, they stuffed ballot boxes with fraudulent votes. In Leavenworth alone, five times as many votes were cast as settlers living in the area. Because of these illegal activities, pro-slavery men gained control of the legislature. They quickly passed laws allowing slavery in Kansas.

Outraged at being denied a fair vote at the polls, those opposed to slavery refused to recognize the territory's new government. Instead, they formed their own legislature to meet in Topeka.

One of the men chosen for this legislature was Isaac Cody. Since the stabbing, he'd gained hero status among antislavery men. Many declared his wounds "the first blood [shed] in the cause of freedom in Kansas." Isaac Cody hadn't considered himself a political man when he first arrived in Kansas, but events had pushed him into taking a stand. When the legislative sessions began in the spring of 1856, Isaac rode the sixty miles to Topeka. He left his family behind.

WILL VERSUS PANTHERS AND NEIGHBORS

"You will have to be the man of the house until my return," Isaac had told his ten-year-old son before he'd left. "But I know I can trust my boy."

It was a heavy responsibility. But Will promised to do his best.

His best meant taking care of the farm. Will and Julia plowed ten acres with their ponies and planted corn. "Willie drove the ponies and I held the plow," remembered Julia. "All that seen [us] said we was doing a good job . . . [Then] Willie dropped the corn and I covered it with the hoe."

That spring, too, Will milked the cows and fetched slopping buckets of water from the nearby spring. He chopped wood and mended fences.

His best also meant looking out for his sisters. According to family legend, one morning little Helen and Eliza wandered across the fields picking wildflowers. Turk trotted along beside them. But as they neared the woods, the dog suddenly grew restless. A ridge of fur stood up on his back. He growled. Moments later, the shrill scream of a panther echoed through the trees.

"With the heart of a lion," Helen later wrote, "[Turk] put himself on guard." The panther crept from the woods. Spying Turk, the big cat sprang. "With a scream such as I never heard from a dog before or after, our defender hurled himself upon the foe."

But Turk was no match for the panther. Within minutes, the dog lay stunned and bleeding. Now the panther turned its glinting eyes on the little girls. "We scarcely dared to breathe," remembered Helen, "and every throb of our frightened little hearts was a prayer that Will would come."

Their prayers were answered. Seconds later there came a "rifle's sharp retort." The panther fell to the ground, and the girls rushed into their brother's arms. Then together they picked up Turk, whose injuries were not fatal, and carried him home.

Worse than planting corn or shooting panthers was facing their neighbors' wrath. Isaac's role in the Topeka legislature infuriated the pro-slavery men, and they took their fury out on his family.

"We were almost daily visited by some of the pro-slavery men," remembered Will, "who helped themselves to anything they saw fit, and frequently [forced] my mother and sisters to cook for them . . . Hardly a day passed without some of them inquiring where the old man was, saying they would kill him on sight."

One night a wagon filled with hooting, laughing ruffians rattled up to the Cody house. Reeking of whiskey, they called for Isaac to come out, apparently not knowing he was away.

Mary sent Will for help. A group of workers from Fort Leavenworth was camping near the Cody farm. Hurry, she urged him.

As Will darted through the shadows, Mary bravely went out to meet the ruffians. She told them her husband wasn't there. But, she added, men from Fort Leavenworth were on their way.

At that moment, from the workers' camp, came the sound of shots being fired into the air.

Whipping up their horses, the ruffians tore away. As they did, a barrel rolled out of the wagon. In their haste, they didn't stop to retrieve it.

Later, when Will returned from the workers' camp, he and his mother went to see what the ruffians had left behind. They were shocked to discover a twenty-five-pound keg of gunpowder. The men had planned on blowing up the Cody house, or so they had boasted at the store where they'd bought the powder.

Amid these incidents, spring and summer wore on. The children picked strawberries, gooseberries, and raspberries. The corn grew tall, and the vegetables ripened. "[I] thought Kansas was beautiful," said Julia, "if it was not infested with those pro-slavery men."

FATHER IN THE SHADOWS

Isaac rarely came home now, and when he did he was in constant dread of being murdered. Careful to arrive after dusk when no one could see him, he always left before first light the next morning. He even kept a secret stable deep in the woods, a half mile from the house. Leaving his horse there so his neighbors wouldn't see it in the yard, he crept through shadow and cornfield to spend a few precious hours with his family.

One night in the fall of 1856 he arrived sick. By the next morning he was so ill he could not get out of bed. Lying upstairs, he prayed no one would discover his presence.

But at lunchtime, a man with the last name of Sharpe rode up.

Bursting into the house, he shouted, "I've come to search the house for that abolition[ist] husband of yours!" Then he plopped into a chair and demanded something to eat.

Hoping to keep Sharpe downstairs, Mary started cooking.

As she did, he unsheathed the big bowie knife he carried at his waist. He began sharpening it on the sole of his boot. When he noticed Will watching, he growled, "[This] is to cut the heart out of that Free State father of yours!"

Mary turned to her children. "Julia, you and Willie take the [younger ones] upstairs," she instructed.

The two did as they were told. Behind them they heard their mother putting dishes on the table and telling Sharpe that Isaac had gone to Topeka.

From his sickbed, Isaac had heard every word. Now he whispered to his two older children, "You will have to protect me. Willie, you get your gun . . . and Julia you get that ax. Now if that man starts to come up the stairs, Willie, you shoot him, and Julia, if Willie misses him, you hit him with the ax."

For several long minutes, brother and sister stood poised, weapons raised at the bedroom door. They must have been terrified, not only by the threat to their father but also by the prospect of what they might be required to do. Ears straining, they listened for the thump of boots on the wooden stairs.

It never came. Convinced that Isaac wasn't there, Sharpe finished his food and headed for the door. But on the threshold he stopped and turned. "We will be on the lookout for [your husband] and we will fix him," he threatened. "We are going to kill ever one of these abolitionists until we clear this territory of them."

As the pounding of his horse's hooves faded away, Will and Julia lowered their weapons.

A TERROR-FILLED CHASE

That same fall, pro-slavery men hatched yet another plot to kill Isaac. It was Dr. Hathaway—one of the family's few friendly neighbors—who tipped off Mary. Border ruffians, he told her, were waiting to ambush Isaac on his return from Grasshopper Falls, a town some thirty miles from the Cody farm. He urged her to get word to her husband that he should not come home.

Will happened to be lying in bed with the flu, vomiting and dizzy, his body racked with chills. Still, he flung off his blankets when he heard the doctor. "I'm going to warn Father," he said.

Mary argued. How could she send a sick child on such a long ride in the middle of the night?

But Will insisted.

While he dressed, Julia hurried out to the barn to saddle Prince and Mary wrote a letter to Isaac explaining the danger.

Tucking the message into his sock before pulling on his boots, the sick boy stumbled outside and climbed onto his pony. He headed off into the darkness.

He did not go fast. He felt too ill for that. Instead, keeping Prince at an easy gait, he sucked in the crisp night air in hopes of settling his stomach.

Eight miles out, at Stranger Creek, he came upon a camp.

One of the men there caught sight of him. "There's Cody's kid!" he cried. "Stop you, and tell us where your old man is!"

"Let's go for him," shouted another man.

Putting his heels to his pony, the boy galloped away. He knew the men had to catch and saddle their horses, giving him some time to ride to the top of the hill that sloped away from the creek and out onto the prairie. Only in that wide, open space might he have a chance to escape.

Will's desperate ride to save his father's life is illustrated in this woodcut from Cody's 1879 autobiography.

Within minutes, several men were galloping after him. Sick and scared, Will pushed his pony to the limit. The two pounded across the open range, their pursuers just a few hundred feet behind.

Will knew he could never outrace them all the way to Grasshopper Falls. What to do? He remembered a family friend, Mr. Hewitt, who owned a big farm just nine miles away. Will would be safe there, if he could make it without getting caught.

For the entire nine miles, Will rode in terror. Behind him he could hear the men's curses and the thundering of their horses' hooves. Ahead of him stretched an endless expanse of darkness. The wind kicked up, seizing the hat from his head and buffeting his weak body. Time and again, he leaned over Prince's heaving neck to vomit. He could barely keep his saddle.

At last, a welcome light gleamed in the darkness. The Hewitt farm!

Coaxing one last burst from his now exhausted pony, Will charged through the farm's open gate and reined up at the house just seconds ahead of the men.

His would-be assassins brought their horses to a quick stop. They didn't want to tangle with Hewitt and his farmhands. Turning, they hightailed it away.

Meanwhile, Will drooped over his pony's neck. He was safe, for now.

All the commotion brought Hewitt from the house with rifle and lantern. He peered into the darkness. "Why, what is this?"

Will barely had the strength to explain. Still, he insisted on continuing to Grasshopper Falls. His father was in danger.

But Hewitt stopped him. He'd seen Isaac just that morning, he said, and he knew for a fact that Will's father would not be heading home until the weekend. There was plenty of time to rest *and* relay the message.

Dragging the sick boy off his pony, he sent him to bed. Then he called a stable hand to care for Prince. The poor animal was not only foaming at the mouth and covered with lather but also flecked with Will's vomit.

The next morning, Will awoke feeling much better. Prince, too, appeared rejuvenated. So after breakfast, the two traveled the remaining thirteen miles to Grasshopper Falls. Pride must have welled up in Will when he finally handed Isaac his mother's message. He had risked his life to save the person he described as "dearer to me than any other man in the world."

SAVING PRINCE

Their neighbors' persecution continued. "They drove off all our stock, and killed our pigs and even the chickens," recalled Will.

They stole Julia's pony, Dolly, too. "I was left without anything to ride, or [any way] to go to the store . . . [I] felt all broke up," she said.

This constant raiding reduced the family to "utter destitution," said Will. "Our only food was what rabbits and birds I could catch with the help of our faithful old dog, Turk." Isaac could not help his family anymore. "His presence, in fact," Will continued, "was merely a menace."

So in early 1857 Isaac left Kansas. He headed east to Ohio, where he made speeches in churches and at town meetings about the beauty of Kansas. His purpose was to recruit new settlers for the territory—all of them against slavery.

Not long after he left, border ruffians swept down on the Cody place yet again. This time they stole Prince. When Will discovered the empty stable, he cried. "The loss of my faithful pony nearly broke my heart," he said. He was convinced he'd never see his friend again.

But just weeks later, as he walked to the fort, he saw something strange—notices fluttering from fence posts and trees. Stranger still was what the notices said. The Kickapoo Rangers, a group of border ruffians, were disbanding for the winter and returning to Missouri. Unable to take along all the horses they'd stolen, they were inviting folks to come and claim their property.

Notice in hand, Will set out for the rangers' camp. Was he concerned about walking into their midst? Apparently not. He was determined to get Prince back.

At their camp, Will looked for his pony. He saw dozens of horses, but none of them were Prince. Still, he was sure the animal was there. So, putting his fingers in his mouth, he whistled sharply.

From behind a closed and locked stall door came an answering whinny.

Prince!

Will hurried to the captain of the rangers. Holding out the notice, he said, "I came to get my pony."

The captain peered down at the boy. "Can you prove you have a horse here?"

"Yes sir," Will replied. "If you will . . . open the door to stall 10 . . . I will show you."

The captain agreed, and Will whistled for Prince again.

"The horse, he whinered, and Willie whistled again," wrote Julia years later. "Prince kicked up and made a jump and started for Willie and got to him and began to fondle around him as much as a person could."

Prince kneeled down as he'd been trained, and Will climbed onto his back. He nudged the pony forward.

That's when the captain, impressed by Will's horse skills and bravery, called after them. He wanted to know the boy's name.

"William F. Cody," said Will proudly.

Then boy and pony rode home together.

CHILDHOOD'S END

Just weeks later, Isaac returned to Salt Creek Valley. He brought along sixty free-soil families he'd recruited in the east. And he'd invited them all to make his home their headquarters. "As a result," remembered Helen, "our house overflowed while the land above us was dotted with tents; but these melted away as one by one the families selected claims and put up cabins."

In March, measles broke out in the settlers' camp, killing four people. Isaac helped bury one of these victims—a little girl—in the cold rain. The next day he came down with a severe chill. Mary sent for Dr. Hathaway, but the physician could do nothing. Isaac's condition worsened, and pneumonia set in. On March 10, 1857, at the age of forty-five, Isaac Cody died.

He left his family penniless.

And he left his son feeling scared and vulnerable. Unlike the brave hero of his later performances, Will Cody the child had not been able to drive the attackers away from his family's cabin. They'd stolen almost everything and, to his mind, killed his father. The future must have looked bleak.

What could he—a skinny eleven-year-old boy—possibly do?

"I made up my mind to be [the] breadwinner," he said.

A reenactment of an attack on a wagon train (c. 1894). The horses were trained to roll onto their sides and play dead.

ACT TWO

BOY ON THE PLAINS
OR
"ILLUSTRATING A PRAIRIE [WAGON] TRAIN CROSSING THE PLAINS—IT IS ATTACKED BY MARAUDING INDIANS WHO ARE IN TURN REPULSED BY BUFFALO BILL AND A NUMBER OF SCOUTS AND COWBOYS."

—Buffalo Bill's Wild West Program, 1894

A SCENE FROM THE WILD WEST

It happens early in the program, just after a shooting exhibition and a horse race. At the far end of the arena a wooden gate is drawn back and a line of covered wagons rides slowly, wearily across the dusty showground. Wooden wheels creek. Canvas snaps in the breeze. Exhausted-looking women and children peek out the back of the wagons. From the driver's seats, men crack their bullwhips above the lumbering oxen and holler, "Whoa! Haw!" Alongside trots a faithful watchdog.

But as the wagon train rolls along, a Lakota scout—then another, and another—appears. They crouch. They watch. They spring. Riding bareback and shrieking, they surround and attack the train. Shots ring out. Arrows slice through the air. One Lakota warrior hurls a flaming torch. Within seconds, columns of black smoke curl toward the sky. One of the wagons is on fire!

People sitting in the front rows can feel the heat coming off the burning canvas. But they don't complain. They believe they are seeing an authentic re-creation of vanishing frontier life. And they are thrilled. Wide-eyed, they watch as the train's women and children take cover behind a wagon that has overturned in the chaos. Meanwhile, the men take aim at their attackers. They shoot. But the odds are against them. The folks on the wagon train are outnumbered. Surrounded.

Then the clarion notes of a trumpet pierce the air. And in swoops Buffalo Bill along with a party of rescuers, firing as they come. The skirmish is surprisingly brief. Beaten back, the Lakota gallop away.

Cries of "Hooray!" and "Bravo!" ring through the smoky air as applause from the audience builds louder and louder. After a gallant bow, Buffalo Bill and his party also ride away. Only the people on the wagon train remain. They snuff out the last of the flames and right their overturned wagon. Then slowly, wearily, they resume their lonely travel.

The audience gives their performance a standing ovation.

William Cody knew about life on a wagon train. He'd spent almost two years of his boyhood rolling across the Great Plains behind a team of oxen. And while he never actually drove away an American Indian war party (attacks of this sort on wagon trains were extremely rare), he *did* face other dangers and hardships. Stampedes. Starvation. Guerrilla soldiers.

He experienced them all before his thirteenth birthday.

HARDSCRABBLE DAYS

On the day after Isaac Cody's funeral, eleven-year-old Will and Julia, just days shy of her fourteenth birthday, sat down at the kitchen table. Their oldest sister, Martha, had gone to work her own claim, but that left four little ones still at home. "[We] planned what must be done to take care of Mother and the three sisters and little brother Charlie [who had been born in May 1855]," Julia recalled. In those days, families that lost their male breadwinners could easily sink into poverty. There were no social safety nets—no widow's pensions, welfare programs, or Social Security. And since society discouraged women from working outside the home, Mary Cody could not seek a paying job. So what could they do? There was only one choice. "I would do all the heavy work of milking and tending the farm, while Will went to work," said Julia.

At that time, the biggest employer in the area was Russell, Majors, and Waddell, a freight and transport company headquartered in Leavenworth. Supplying military posts in Colorado and Utah with necessary goods, it shipped millions of pounds of food, clothing, and ammunition by wagon train every year. To accomplish this, the company was said to employ forty thousand oxen and six thousand men.

Will hoped to become the company's six thousand and first employee. Saddling up Prince, he rode into town, where he asked Alexander Majors for a job.

Majors, who'd been on friendly terms with Isaac Cody, wanted to help. But the boy who stood before him was just a "wiry, little lad," he recalled. What could he possibly do?

"I can ride as well as a man," Will told him.

Impressed by the boy's confidence, if not his size, Majors consulted with one of the other partners in the firm, William Russell. Still doubtful, they finally offered him a job as an express boy. His duties were to carry messages between the firm's headquarters in town and the telegraph office at Fort Leavenworth, three miles away.

Will jumped at the offer. He was assigned a company mule and told to report at eight o'clock sharp the next morning.

Arriving the following day bright and early, Will received his first message.

"Go and come as quickly as you can," Russell instructed.

Will did as he was told, racing to the fort and back.

He was so quick that when he walked into Russell's office just a short time later, the man frowned. "Have you not gone yet?" he scolded.

In reply, the boy placed the answer to the message on Russell's desk.

The man couldn't believe it. He praised Will's speediness. Then, jokingly, he cautioned him not to "ride all my mules to death."

"No, sir, I will not," Will promised solemnly.

The eleven-year-old carried messages for the next two months. But there was too much sitting around offices and too little riding to suit him. So he asked Majors for a transfer. Soon he went to work with John Willis, one of the company's wagon train bosses, helping herd the company oxen. During those weeks on the range, Will moved livestock and perfected his lassoing skills. He also learned to shoot with a pistol. When the job ended, Willis—who'd grown fond of the boy— gave Will a revolver of his own. Will returned home with it strapped around his waist. Strutting around the Cody house, he acted "big," recalled Julia.

His mother quickly put him back in his place. Taking away the pistol, she told Will the good news. He was going back to school!

Will resisted. Why should he spend his days cooped up inside a classroom when the outdoors was such an excellent school? He'd already acquired a great deal of practical knowledge from his jobs. What could be more valuable than that? Besides, his family couldn't possibly get along without his wages.

Mary Cody waved aside his arguments. A new school had opened up in the neighborhood, and she insisted he attend. Worried about Will's lack of education, she'd sold some of the family's farmland. The cash she'd received would see them through the coming months while the boy attended class.

Now every morning Will trudged across the meadow to the log school-house. His sisters Helen and Eliza went along, too. But not Julia. "I, of course, could not go as there was no one to do the chores and house-work," she sadly recalled. Four-year-old May also stayed home.

Will would have preferred helping around the house. Paying little attention to his lessons, he daydreamed about shooting guns and riding the open plains. "The master of the school wore out several arm-fuls of hazel switches in a vain attempt to teach me the three R's," he admitted.

Weeks passed, and despite himself Will began making progress in his studies. Then in August 1857 he developed a crush on a girl. And, he confessed, it "blasted my prospects for acquiring an education."

His sweetheart was Mary Hyatt, with whom he was "dead in love." But he had a rival for Mary's affections, a boy three years older named Steve Gobel, "the bully of the school."

In those days, boys built little playhouses in the trees and bushes for their sweethearts, and Will made one for Mary.

Jealous, Steve Gobel pushed it over.

Will went after the older boy with his fists but was sent sprawling by a punch to the jaw. Steve leaped on top of him.

That's when the teacher came running from the schoolhouse. Breaking up the fight, he marched the boys inside, where he paddled them both. "This made matters worse than ever," admitted Will. "I had received two thrashings to Steve's one."

Will smothered his angry feelings as best he could and, during afternoon recess, built Mary another little house. Once again, Steve demolished it.

Will looked his rival in the eye. "The next time you do that," he threatened, "I'll hurt you."

Steve just laughed.

The next morning, Will began building yet another playhouse. But he was only half done when Steve knocked it over yet again.

Will saw red. Reaching into his boot, he grabbed the penknife he always carried there. Flicking open the blade, he thrust it into Steve's thigh.

It wasn't a deep wound, but it bled a lot.

"I am killed!" shrieked Steve. "Oh, I am killed!"

Their classmates raced over. Terrified by the scene, many started crying. "[Willie] Cody has murdered Steve Gobel. Steve is dead!"

Steve wasn't dead, just bleeding. The commotion brought the teacher on the run. He had "vengeance in his eye and a big club in his hand," remembered Will.

What else could the boy do?

He ran.

And he kept on running until he reached a freight wagon train being led by his old friend John Willis.

Panting, Will spilled out the story. "[Steve's] friends will . . . soon be looking for me," he cried when he finished.

Willis hid the boy under the canvas cover of his wagon. Minutes later, Steve's father and the local constable stormed up the dirt road. They'd seen Will headed in the direction of the wagon train and were coming to arrest him.

"We want [Will Cody]," Mr. Gobel growled at Willis.

John Willis asked if they had an arrest warrant.

The constable admitted they didn't.

"Well, you can't get him," said Willis. "That settles it."

Gobel argued. But Willis refused to give in. Eventually, the men left.

Will then crept out of his hiding place. Was he really going to jail?

"Come along with me," suggested Willis. He was headed to Fort

This daguerreotype of twelve-year-old Will was taken around the time of his first wagon train trip across the plains.

Kearny, in Nebraska, and expected the trip to take forty days. By that time, the wagon master figured, the wounded boy would have recovered and all the excitement would have died down.

Will agreed. That night, under cover of darkness, he crept home and told his mother about Willis's plan. Reluctantly, Mary Cody gave her permission. After all, she reasoned, her son was better off working on a wagon train than sitting in jail.

And so, "kissing her and my sisters a fond farewell," remembered Will, "I started off on my first trip across the plains, and with a light heart, too, notwithstanding my trouble of a few hours before."

As for his sweetheart, Mary Hyatt, he apparently didn't give her a second thought.

STAMPEDE!

Will described a freight wagon train this way:

> The wagons used in those days . . . were known as "J. Murphy wagons," made at St. Louis specially for the plains business.

They were very large and were strongly built, being capable of carrying seven thousand pounds of freight each. The wagon boxes were very commodious—being as large as the rooms of an ordinary house—and were covered with two heavy canvas sheets to protect the merchandise from the rain. These wagons were . . . each drawn by several yokes of oxen in [the] charge of one driver. A train consisted of twenty-five wagons, all in [the] charge of one man known as the wagon-master. The second man in command was the assistant wagon-master; then came the "extra hand," next the night herder; and lastly, the cavallard driver [Will's job], whose duty it was to drive the lame and loose cattle. There were thirty-one men all told in a train. The men did their own cooking, being divided into messes of seven. One man cooked, another brought water and wood, another stood guard, and so on, each having some duty to perform while getting meals. All were heavily armed . . . and every one always had his weapons handy so as to be prepared for any emergency.

Slowly, the wagon train moved through hills and plains. Near the Platte River in Nebraska, it came upon its first herd of buffalo. The shaggy creatures were calmly grazing between the trail and the river about two miles away. Will, who'd never seen a buffalo before, was fascinated. With their humped backs and short, stubby legs they appeared clumsy and slow.

He soon learned otherwise. A group of hunters suddenly galloped over the ridge and dashed down on the herd. The frightened buffalo broke for the trail where Willis's wagons rolled along. "About five hundred of them rushed [toward] our train pell mell," wrote Will. The stampeding animals were on them so quickly that Willis's men could do nothing but duck behind the biggest wagons. Recalled Will, "Some of the wagons were turned clear around, and many of the terrified oxen attempted to run to the hills, with the heavy wagons attached to them . . . Nearly all the teams got entangled in their gearing, and became wild with [fear] . . . The buffaloes, the cattle, and the [men] were soon running in every direction."

The stampede lasted only a few minutes. But it took three days to round up the oxen and repair the wagons. Then, once again, the train moved along the trail toward Fort Kearny. Luckily, recalled Will, the remainder of the trip was "enjoyable . . . no incidents worthy of note occurred on the way."

The train averaged a dozen miles a day on the trip out when the wagons were loaded to the tops of the canvas covers. Without cargo, it made the return trip at twice the speed. Good thing, because Will was eager to get home, even though it meant facing the Gobel family's fury.

He needn't have worried. While he was gone, Mary Cody had made peace with Steve and his father. Will no longer faced the prospect of jail. In fact, he and Steve eventually became friends. "We have had many a laugh together over our love affair and the affray at the schoolhouse," Will later said.

MORMON WARS AND A STARVATION WINTER

Will did not stay put for long. He claimed that just days after his return, he signed up with wagon master Lew Simpson's outfit. It was headed for Salt Lake City with a herd of cattle to supply the U.S. Army.

Mary had felt torn about giving her permission. The boy belonged in school. He could barely write his name. And yet the family once again needed his wages. The money she'd received from the sale of their farmland was gone, and the Codys were close to penniless once more. Reluctantly, she let her son go.

On this trip the eleven-year-old worked as a boy extra, riding from wagon to wagon, relaying orders. "Everything ran along smoothly with us . . . until we came within about eighteen miles of Green River, in the Rocky Mountains," Will later claimed. The wagon train stopped to water the cattle at a nearby creek. As was usual, most of the crew crawled under the wagons to escape the heat of the day. Covering their faces with their hats, they napped.

While they slept, a hundred armed men on horseback quickly surrounded the wagons. At gunpoint, they disarmed the still-groggy crew. Their leader rode forward. It was Lot Smith, commander of the Mormon Raiders.

Just months earlier and for political reasons, President James Buchanan had decided to replace Brigham Young—president of a religious group called the Church of Jesus Christ of Latter-Day Saints, more commonly known as Mormons—as acting governor of the Utah Territory. Anticipating an angry reaction, Buchanan had also sent twenty-five hundred soldiers to Utah to ensure his orders were carried out.

Young feared the worst. Ten years earlier he had led his people to Salt Lake City after angry mobs in Illinois had burned Mormon homes and murdered church leaders. He worried this would happen again in Utah. "Woe, woe, to that man who comes here to . . . meddle with me and this people," he said. He responded to the president by forming a new guerrilla organization called the Mormon Raiders. Rather than fighting the U.S. Army directly, the Mormon Raiders attacked its supply trains. Without provisions, the Raiders hoped, Buchanan's troops would be forced to leave Utah.

Now Lot Smith turned to wagon boss Lew Simpson and said, "I intend to burn your train."

"[And] turn us adrift here?" cried Simpson. How would his men survive in the middle of the wilderness without food or weapons?

Smith relented. He allowed Simpson's crew six yoke of oxen and one wagon with enough provisions to last until they reached Fort Bridger, hundreds of miles away.

But how were his men supposed to get to the fort? asked Simpson.

"On foot," replied Smith.

As the dejected wagon crew began their long trek to Fort Bridger, they looked back. Smoke and fire rose to the sky. Their train had gone up in flames.

"There was nothing to do but walk," claimed Will.

They reached Fort Bridger in November 1857. The place was little more than a collection of rough-hewn log buildings. Partially burned by Mormons just weeks earlier, it provided poor shelter to those who gathered there. Besides Simpson's thirty-five men, there were crews from two other captured wagon trains as well as U.S. troops who'd been forced to stop there for the winter.

Winter settled in with bone-scraping winds and plummeting temperatures. The shivering men scoured the countryside for firewood and sagebrush. When blizzards heaped up mountains of snow and made paths impassable, they burned wagons, sleds, furniture—anything to keep warm.

Food was scarcer than fuel. That's because Mormon militiamen surrounded the fort, cutting off suppliers. Before the winter ended, men were put on three-quarter rations. This was soon reduced to half rations, and finally one-quarter rations. With no other choice, the men killed their animals. The oxen were so weak, said Will, "that we had to prop them up to shoot them down . . . It was really a serious state of affairs."

When the snow finally melted, Will and the teamsters headed home. On the way they stopped at Fort Laramie, in what is now eastern Wyoming, where the bone-thin boy drank coffee and wolfed down hardtack, bacon, and beans. "I can honestly say I thought it was the best meal I had ever eaten," he asserted more than thirty years later.

✧ PANNING FOR THE TRUTH ✦
THE MORMON WAR

Yarns. Half-truths. Exaggerations. That's what historians have called some of Will Cody's boyhood stories. Will had a tendency, when looking back on his early years, to embellish events. So how can we believe anything he said about that time? By comparing his claims to other historical records.

The most important of these records is his sister Julia's memoir. She, too, wrote about Will's childhood. But she stuck to the truth even when it contradicted her brother's more imaginary accounts. How do we know? Because her memoir checks out against dozens of other historical records. And for the most part, her recollections support Will's. That is, until his adventure in the 1857 Mormon War.

Some historians have questioned whether Will really was with the Utah expedition that winter. They cite as proof his lack of details about both the trip and his time at Fort Bridger. He spent almost a year away from home and in that time would have met plenty of generals and soldiers, not to mention every boy's hero in those days—the legendary mountain man Jim Bridger. Bridger was the expedition's chief guide and scout. But Will—who enjoyed bragging about his friendships with famous frontiersmen—never mentioned Bridger, not once. Instead, he noted meeting just one character, James Butler "Wild Bill" Hickok. Too bad Hickok wasn't in Utah at that time. According to letters Hickok wrote to his family, he was farming in Kansas.

Julia claims Will was in Kansas, too. That winter "Willie and I would take the pony team and . . . get wood . . . ," she wrote. "[We] spent a lot of time in hunting . . . rabbits, squirrels and prairie chickens and had traps to catch quail."

Will didn't dispute her recollection. Years later when he read her account, he remarked, "Say, that write up of yours was fine. You have a wonderful memory."

So could it be that Will's was simply faulty?

Some historians doubt it. "A bright, keen-memoried eleven-year-old should have retained a myriad of indelible impressions . . . The only explanation for such amnesia . . . is that he [never made] the journey," remarked one. They believe Will fabricated the story in later years to spice up his reputation as a frontiersman.

But other historians are not so sure. After all, a scrap of historical evidence supporting the story does exist. In 1901, a soldier from the First U.S. Cavalry verified the boy's presence at Fort Bridger. "He . . . impressed me as a rather fresh, 'smart-ellick' sort of kid," remembered the soldier. "[A] little, dirty-faced bull-whacker" who was "quite a pet" of the wagon crew.

But is this single account enough to prove Will *was* there?

The debate continues.

WILL GETS SCHOOLED

Since there was no neighborhood school in the spring of 1858, twelve-year-old Will spent his time back in Kansas cutting and hauling wood for pay, and hunting with Turk. In his free time, he roughhoused with little Charlie and played with his younger sisters. But after so many adventures on the trail, it was hard to return to ordinary family life. "My restless, roaming spirit would not allow me to remain at home very long," Will admitted.

In September, he signed up with a wagon train headed to Fort Laramie. An old frontier post, Fort Laramie served the needs of the thousands of emigrants who traveled westward along the Oregon and California trails. A bustling place, it boasted stores, a hospital, and blacksmith and carpenter shops, as well as neat adobe barracks and officers' quarters built around a large parade ground. Outside its protective walls lived three or four thousand Native people, and Will found time to play with Cheyenne, Arapaho, and Sioux children. "The wagon beds became splendid playhouses," recalled Will. "[And] I joined them in their games, and from them picked up a fair working knowledge of the Sioux language."

The boy loitered at the fort, trapping beaver and otter, and making a brief trip to Cheyenne Pass, some one hundred miles away, to supply a new post being established there. But by January 1859, he was ready to go home. Hitching himself to a return outfit, he headed back to Leavenworth. He arrived four weeks later.

"I had nearly a thousand dollars to turn over to my mother as soon as I should draw my pay," Will recalled.

Proud of this accomplishment, he took Mary Cody along on payday. He wanted her to see Alexander Majors hand over that thick stack of bills. He just knew the sight would make her proud.

Instead, she burst into tears.

Will asked why she was crying.

"You couldn't even write your name, Willie," she sobbed. "You couldn't sign the payroll. To think my boy cannot so much as write his name!"

Will had never considered school important. But now, he said, "I thought about [Mother's words] all the way home."

Back to school he went.

"At last, I really began to take an interest," he said. He worked especially hard at learning to write. With the burnt end of a stick, he practiced his penmanship on every available surface—tents, wagon covers, ox yokes, trees, and barn doors. The words "Will Cody," "Little Billy," "Willy the messenger boy," and "William Frederic[k] Cody," were "plastered pretty well over the whole of Salt Creek Valley," confessed the boy. He was soon writing his name instead of signing an *X* to the payroll.

Two Boys Go Hunting

Will was also planning his next adventure. This time he decided to try his luck as a fur trapper. So in November 1859, he and his friend Dave Harrington headed out with an ox-drawn wagon full of provisions and traps. At the mouth of Prairie Dog Creek, on the border of Kansas and Nebraska, the two teenagers pitched camp. They built a dugout in a nearby hillside and covered it with brush and long grass. Inside they constructed a fireplace for cooking and heating, while outside they built a corral for the ox.

The weeks swept by. During the day, the boys busied themselves baiting the traps for beaver and otter, skinning off pelts, and salting the hides before storing them away. At night they sat beside the fire swapping stories until they fell asleep, the coyotes wailing in the distance.

One night, as they were dozing off, they heard a commotion in the corral. Grabbing a rifle, Dave rushed from the dugout and found himself face-to-face with a bear. He fired.

With a howl, the furious and wounded bear charged.

Will, who was just rounding the corner of the dugout, lifted his rifle to his shoulder. "I took the best aim I could in the dark," he recalled, "and the bear . . . rolled over dead."

The ox was dead, too. "We were now left without a team [to pull the wagon]; and two hundred miles from home," said Will. Still, the pelts were piling up. The boys decided to stick it out until spring, when one of them would walk to the nearest settlement for help.

Unfortunately, this plan was put into action much sooner than expected. Just days later, the boys spied a herd of elk. They stalked the animals along an ice-covered creek. Crouching to get a good shot, Will slipped. "'Snap!' went something," he later recalled. It was his leg, broken just above the ankle.

Dave managed to half drag, half carry his pain-racked friend back to the dugout. Using a wagon bow, he splinted the fracture. "[Then he] placed me on our little bunk with plenty of blankets to cover me," Will later wrote. "[My] provisions he put within my reach. A cup was lashed to a long sapling, and Harrington made a hole in the side of the dugout so that I could reach the cup out to a snow-bank for my water supply. Lastly, he cut a great pile of wood and heaped it near the fire. Without leaving my bunk I could thus do a little cooking, keep the fire up and eat and sleep." When all was ready, Dave went for help. He figured it would take twenty days to get to the nearest town and back.

The lonely days crept by. To mark them off, Will cut notches in a big stick. On the fourteenth day of his confinement, it began to snow. The drifts grew deeper and deeper until they sealed off the dugout's entrance, burying the dwelling under three feet of snow. He could hear a pack of snarling, howling wolves, drawn by the smell of his food, scratching at the snow-packed doorway. Will's mind filled with dark imaginings. What if Dave had been killed on the trail? What if he was snowbound, unable to bring help? What if the wolves got to him before Dave did?

The notches on the stick multiplied.

Twenty cuts, and no Dave.

Twenty-one, and still no Dave.

Twenty-two, and Will remained alone.

"I had nearly given up all hopes of leaving the dugout alive," he recalled.

At last, on the twenty-ninth day, he heard Dave shouting, "Whoa! Haw!" to his oxen and calling out Will's name.

"I was so glad to see him that I put my arms around his neck and hugged him for five minutes," admitted Will.

Dave loaded up their traps and furs, then arranged a bed in the wagon for the injured boy. After eight days of pushing through snow, they arrived at a farmhouse, where they rested for two days before heading on to the farm where Dave had borrowed the team. From there they traveled to Junction City, where they sold the furs and the wagon, then joined up with a government mule team headed for Fort Leavenworth. They arrived home in March 1860.

Grateful for all he'd done, Mary Cody asked Dave to stay with them. Without family of his own, Dave agreed, and he and Will began making plans to work the Codys' land. No more wagon trains or messenger jobs. They would make a go of the farm and share the financial responsibilities. For the first time since his father's death, Will felt safe and happy. But just weeks later, Dave became seriously ill and, despite Mary Cody's motherly care, died.

Will was heartbroken. He had lost his best friend, the companion who had saved his life. "I felt very lonely without [Dave]," he said, "and I soon wished for a change of scene again."

A modern-day performer reenacts the speed and skill of a Pony Express rider.

ACT
THREE

THE YOUNGEST RIDER ON THE PONY EXPRESS
OR
"PONY EXPRESS—THE FORMER PONY [EXPRESS] RIDER WILL SHOW HOW THE LETTERS AND TELEGRAMS OF THE REPUBLIC WERE DISTRIBUTED ACROSS THE IMMENSE CONTINENT PREVIOUS TO THE BUILDING OF RAILWAYS AND TELEGRAPHS."

—Buffalo Bill's Wild West Program, 1894

A SCENE FROM THE WILD WEST

Horse and rider burst into the arena. There is a cloud of dust, a pounding of hooves as they charge toward a log cabin—a Pony Express station—placed in the center of the showground. Before it stands a man holding the reins of a second pony.

Nearing the cabin, the rider flings himself from his horse while still moving at full speed. The audience gasps. Incredibly . . . impossibly . . . the rider snatches his mochila—*a special Pony Express saddle cover with four locking mail pockets—from the still-moving steed. In one seemingly effortless motion, he tosses it over the saddle of the second horse, then springs onto the horse's back.*

In a flash they are off, the new horse charging around the arena, the rider bent low over its neck, the wind whipping both hair and mane. They are racing time, reenacting the crossing of the country, a man alone on the back of a galloping horse.

They come to a second log cabin, a second station man, another waiting horse. Once again, the rider performs the impossible. Do his boots even touch the ground?

The audience is standing now, clapping and whistling, as the rider thunders toward yet a third station. Most cannot believe their eyes. What skill! What speed! What a showstopper!

Horse and rider race around the arena one last time. The audience cheers. They love a race. They love a winner. And they love the glorious memory of the Pony Express.

Most showgoers never questioned Cody's claims of riding the Pony Express. Why should they? The words were printed right there in the Wild West program. "[He] . . . was employed as a herder, wagonmaster, and pony express rider," the biography section of the sixty-plus-page booklet read. Those eager to know more could buy Cody's autobiography at the bookstall on the showgrounds. For just two dollars, they could read all about his express-riding derring-do: American Indian raids and outlaw skirmishes, record-breaking trips and remarkable endurance. "Even now my heart echoes the fading, distant hoof beats of the Pony Express," said Will in later life.

And some of those hoofbeats might even have been real.

"PIKE'S PEAK OR BUST!"

The spring of 1860 dragged into summer. Fourteen-year-old Will hobbled around the farm on a set of crutches, waiting for his leg to heal. He felt miserable. He missed Dave. And he longed for a new adventure. But what? The wagons rolling westward along the Salt Creek Trail soon gave him an idea. Some boasted signs that read "Pike's Peak or Bust!" Will knew what that meant. A year earlier, gold had been found at Pikes Peak on the eastern edge of the Rocky Mountains. Already, thousands of people had flocked to Colorado in hopes of striking it rich. And more were headed there every day. Just as his father had years earlier, Will caught gold fever.

He was still limping that June morning when he kissed his family goodbye and joined a wagon train bound for Denver. From there, he and a buddy—fifteen-year-old Pat Patterson—pushed on for the gold streams in the mountains. They settled in a rough-and-tumble mining camp called Black Hawk.

A glimpse of what Will and his friend Pat Patterson experienced. This photograph, c.1870, shows miners and a mule toiling away at an underground gold vein in Black Hawk, Colorado.

Here they spent the next two months panning, digging, and growing deeper in debt. Although Black Hawk was little more than a collection of tents and shacks, prices for everything from bread to barbering were exorbitant. A person couldn't afford to live there unless his pockets were filled with gold nuggets. But the teenagers hadn't found a single flake. "We soon concluded that prospecting . . . was not our forte," said Will.

It was time to go home. But how? The boys couldn't pay for their return trip. They didn't have a dollar between them. According to both Pat Patterson and Julia Cody, they solved this problem by hiring themselves out on a wagon train headed for Kansas. They reached home in November 1860.

Will, however, told a different story.

"The happy thought of constructing a small raft—which would float us clear to the Missouri [River] and thence down to Leavenworth—entered our heads," Will wrote in his 1879 autobiography. After stocking the raft with provisions, he claimed, he and Pat soon pushed off along the South Platte River.

All went well at first. Then near the town of Julesburg, Colorado, disaster struck: "Our raft got caught in an eddy, and quick as lightning went to pieces, throwing us into the stream, which was so deep we had to swim ashore. We lost everything we had."

Boots squelching, the boys walked into town. Incredibly, they soon bumped into an old friend of Will's named George Chrisman. Formerly a wagon master, Chrisman was now working as a station man for Russell, Majors, and Waddell's newest venture—the Pony Express.

The Pony Express had been born of necessity. By 1860, half a million people lived beyond the Rocky Mountains. But St. Joseph, Missouri, was as far west as either the railroad or the telegraph reached. Beyond this point lay a forbidding landscape—endless prairie, raging rivers, rugged mountains. So how to deliver the mail? Letters typically took a month to reach California by boat. An early attempt using mules had a delivery time of fifty-three days from Salt Lake City to Sacramento. And stagecoaches—the fastest of the three methods—took twenty-four days between St. Louis and San Francisco. Russell, Majors, and Waddell devised a plan to cut that time in half: twelve days from St. Louis (fourteen in the snow).

Their idea was to use a mapped-out route with a number of stops, or stations, along the way. Riders would carry the mail from station to station, stopping for a fresh horse at each. Every hundred or so miles, the rider would be replaced. This allowed the mail to move constantly at a fast pace.

The route used by the Pony Express stretched 1,966 miles, from St. Joseph to Sacramento, with 148 stops along the way. It followed the Oregon Trail for a while, then used the Mormon Trail to Salt Lake City before traveling over the Rocky Mountains and Sierra Nevada into California.

Riding the route was hard on both men and horses. Even under the best conditions, a ten- or fifteen-mile run was a grueling experience; a one-hundred-mile nonstop ride was nothing short of torturous. Of the eighty riders employed when the Pony Express began in April 1860, only a few lasted the entire eighteen months of the operation. Some riders arrived at stations bleeding from their noses and mouths. They suffered frostbite from winter's blasts, and temporary blindness from the glaring sun. So dangerous was express riding that Bolivar Roberts, superintendent of the line's western end, supposedly placed this employment ad in a San Francisco newspaper:

> Wanted—young, skinny, wiry fellows, not over 18.
> Must be expert riders, willing to risk death daily.
> Orphans preferred. Wages $25 a week.

This was the job Chrisman offered Will. "He hired me at once . . . ," said Will. "I was required to make fifteen miles an hour, including [three] changes of horses."

What was his route?

Will never said. The only detail he gave about riding for Chrisman was this: "I easily made my forty-five miles on time on my first trip, and ever afterward."

He also never explained what happened to Pat Patterson.

Will stuck with the job for two months. Then a letter from Julia arrived. Mary Cody, suffering with tuberculosis (a disease affecting her lungs), was gravely ill. Julia begged him to come home.

By the time he arrived, his mother's health had improved. Weak but smiling, she greeted him at the door. She hoped he would stay for good.

But as the warm days of summer approached, Will hankered to ride the Pony Express once more. "There's some life in that," he explained.

Mary Cody begged him to abandon the idea. "It [will] surely kill [you]," she said.

But Will refused to be swayed. "I finally convinced her that as I was of no use on the farm, it would be better and more profitable for me to return to the plains."

Once again, he bid farewell to family and farm.

RIDING THE PONY EXPRESS

This time, according to Will, he traveled with a freight outfit to Fort Laramie, Wyoming. He then rode another thirty-six miles west to Horseshoe Station. When he arrived, he boldly walked into the rough-hewn log cabin that served as the Pony Express depot. He asked for a job.

The stationmaster, Joseph Slade, took stock of the skinny fifteen-year-old. "My boy," he said dismissively, "you are too young for a pony express rider."

Will piped up. "I rode two months last year . . . and filled the bill then; and I think I am better able to ride now."

"What?" exclaimed Slade in surprise. "Are you the boy that . . . was called the youngest rider on the road?"

"I am the same boy," Will answered proudly.

Slade immediately offered Will the run from Red Butte west to Three Crossings, a dangerous and lonely seventy-six-mile stretch across Wyoming's barren plains. "It was a long piece of road," Will bragged in his 1879 autobiography, "but I was equal to the undertaking."

One day, just weeks into his new job, Will galloped into the Three Crossings Station. Dusty and tired, he pulled the *mochila* off his saddle, eager to hand it over to the next rider on the run west. As usual, riding full out for seventy-six miles had left him feeling shaken "all to pieces." All he wanted now was a hot meal and some rest. Instead, the stationmaster gave Will some bad news: the next rider, Charles Miller, was dead; he'd been killed the night before in a drunken brawl.

Will had given his word of honor to always move the mail through. So ignoring his weariness, he struggled on. Changing horses, he rode the eighty-five miles to Rocky Ridge. Then, still without rest, he turned around and rode all the way to his home station of Red Butte—a total of 322 miles. It was the third-longest Pony Express ride on record, Will claimed, and he made it in twenty-one hours and forty minutes.

"My boy, you're a brick, and no mistake," Slade declared when he heard about Will's feat.

Will told other tales about riding the Pony Express, too. "A party of fifteen Indians 'jumped me' in a sand ravine about a mile west of the station," he claimed in one story. Putting spurs to his horse, he just managed to escape. Then he charged on toward the Sweetwater Bridge Station, eleven miles away. He was shocked by what he found there. Earlier that day, a band of American Indians had killed the livestock tender and stolen all the horses. Unable to change ponies, he raced on to the next station, making a twenty-four-mile run with just one horse. "I told the people [there] about what had happened at Sweetwater Bridge," he wrote, "then with a fresh [mount] went on and finished the trip without any further adventure."

This was not, said Will, an isolated incident. He claimed that American Indian attacks along the route grew so troublesome that authorities closed down the Pony Express for six weeks. Something had to be done. So Will and a group of express riders, stock tenders, and ranchmen went in search of the raiders. The leader of the search party, he claimed, was none other than the famous gunfighter, gambler, and lawman Wild Bill Hickok.

Twenty miles from the Sweetwater Bridge Station, the men discovered a trail. Following it, they soon came to the raiders' camp. From the opposite side of a creek, Will and the others scouted out their enemy. "We knew full well the Indians would outnumber us three to one," said Will. The men needed a foolproof plan. It was Hickok who suggested they wait until dark and then "make a dash on [the Indian] camp, open a general fire on them, and stampede the horses."

Hickok's plan worked. "The dash . . . was a complete surprise," claimed Will. "We could not have astonished them more if we'd dropped down into their camp from the clouds."

Days later, the men returned to the Sweetwater Bridge Station. With them came all the stolen horses, as well as a hundred more ponies captured from the American Indians. Apparently, no one seemed to think it ironic that they'd become horse thieves themselves. Instead, they thought of the men as heroes. "The recovered horses were replaced on the road, and the . . . pony express [was] again running on time," bragged Will.

✧ PANNING FOR THE TRUTH ✧
THE PONY EXPRESS

Were Will's claims about his Pony Express adventures true? Let's look at a few facts, beginning with his raft trip down the South Platte River. Rafting would have required spending money on building supplies and provisions. But he and Pat Patterson were penniless. So how did the two boys manage it? Will never says.

Additionally, the South Platte in late summer dries up, becoming very shallow. The river, writes one historian, "can scarcely float a bar of soap." Such a trip would have required a "month of miracles."

Will says that at Julesburg his old friend George Chrisman gave him a job riding the ponies. Sadly, company records containing a list of riders do not exist. But the 1860 census does. It notes just Chrisman and two riders—George McGee and Alexander Benham—living at the Julesburg station. The name "William Cody" does not appear anywhere. Historians also wonder how a mere fourteen-year-old convinced Chrisman to give him such a grueling job. And why was a lowly station-master hiring riders in the first place? Only division agents (area supervisors) were permitted to do that. No wonder some historians are skeptical about this story.

They are even more skeptical about Will's second spell of Pony Express riding. Remember Charles Miller, the man killed in a drunken brawl and the reason for Will's incredible nonstop ride? The historical record does show that a man named Charles Miller was killed during a fight in a Wyoming saloon. His murder, however, happened not only at a different station (the Gilbert Station at South Pass) but also on a different date— February 4, 1859—almost a full year before the Pony Express even started. Could Will have simply gotten names and dates mixed up? Or did he, as some historians believe, make up this story later in life to impress his audiences with his mastery of the frontier?

And what about Will's claims that American Indian attacks became so frequent the Pony Express was forced to shut down? Historical records show that the service never once halted operations during its eighteen months in business. Still, Will next claims that he and a group of men, led by none other than Wild Bill Hickok, headed north into American Indian territory to recover the company's stolen horses and get the Pony Express running again. Problem is, Wild Bill Hickok was nowhere near Wyoming at that time. He was tending livestock at a station in faraway Rock Creek in eastern Nebraska. Could Will have been mistaken about who led their group? It's doubtful. It's more likely he wanted to connect his name with the legendary Hickok's.

All this historical evidence suggests that Will's accounts are nothing more than fiction. And yet there is some testimony corroborating his claims. The first comes from a prominent collector of western Americana named Edward Ayer. He recalled: "I crossed the Plains in 1860 . . . and [Cody] was riding by our [wagon] train . . . and call[ed] out the news in a loud voice as he rushed by." While there are some problems with this story—Ayer's wagon route was on the north bank of the Platte River, whereas the Pony Express route was on the south bank—most historians agree that it's not entirely impossible.

A second eyewitness, Pony Express rider Charlie Becker, insisted he and Will became good friends on the route. The snag in this story has to do with dates. Becker said he rode with Will for the entire eighteen months that the Pony Express was in existence. But Will himself wrote that he served on two different sections of the route, and neither time for very long. Could Becker simply be mistaken about the length of time? Again, it's possible.

The final eyewitness was Will's former boss Alexander Majors. In his memoir, *Seventy Years on the Frontier*, Majors verified that Will worked for him on the Pony Express. The boy, he wrote, "was among the most noted and daring riders." Majors, however, wrote his autobiography when he was broke and living in a mining shack outside of Denver. He hoped to make a little money from the book. Will, then at the height of his fame as a showman, wanted to help the man who'd given him his first job as a messenger. So he not only paid to have Majors's autobiography printed but also hired a professional writer to edit it. He even sold the book at his Wild West show, with all the royalties going to Majors.

Could Majors have included the Pony Express story because he felt obligated to Will? Or could Will's writer have added it without Majors's permission? Majors did complain about the writer's embellishment of his facts. The writer, however, argued that he was just trying to tell a good story.

Did Will ride the Pony Express or not?

The question is still being debated. One historian writes, "There seems no point in resisting the inevitable: Bill's pony riding represents another spate of fiction." Yet another writes, "I'm inclined to think that Cody's Pony Express work was real, if possibly exaggerated."

GETTING EVEN

By June 1861, Will was back on the farm—that is, if he'd actually ever left—chopping wood, hunting, and occasionally going to school. "The first rumblings of the great struggle that was soon to be known as the Civil War were reverberating throughout the North," he recalled. Eleven slave states had seceded from the Union. Confederates had fired on Fort Sumter. And in Will's neck of the woods—the border between Kansas and Missouri—savage fighting had broken into the open.

Throughout the 1850s, free-soilers in Kansas had longed for vengeance against their Missouri tormentors. Now they got their chance. Angry men organized themselves into loosely knit private armies with the purpose of "invading Missouri and making war on its people," recalled Will. Acting as guerrillas and without approval from the federal government, these men, known as Jayhawkers, pillaged and murdered their Missouri neighbors. Dragging their enemies from their homes at night, they beat them, cut off their ears, and shot or hanged them. They stole, destroyed, and burned.

In their zeal to punish and plunder, Jayhawkers didn't bother to separate Unionists from Confederates. Recalled Missourian Lizzie Brannock, "[Jayhawkers] came upon us [and] stripped us of nearly everything . . . [even though] we were Union and had never done anything against the government . . . They burned 150 houses, helpless women and children sick were taken out and left standing in the snow while all they owned on earth . . . was destroyed before their eyes."

What happened to Lizzie was repeated again and again across western Missouri. Within ten months, Jayhawkers reduced the once-fertile land around the border to ashes and wilderness. As for the people who'd lived there, many had been murdered. Thousands more had been left homeless and wandering.

"The tables are turned now," said one Kansan after viewing the burned-out wasteland of western Missouri. "[We] are . . . settling up old scores."

Fifteen-year-old Will wanted to settle old scores, too. As far as he was concerned, pro-slavery Missourians had murdered Isaac Cody. They had threatened his mother, sisters, and little brother. "Having a longing and revengeful desire to retaliate . . . for the brutal manner in which they had treated and robbed my family," said Will, "I became a [Jayhawker]."

WILL CODY: HORSE THIEF

On a warm night in June, Will slipped from his house. Riding alone through the shadowy darkness, he headed for a rendezvous spot on the Kansas–Missouri border. Twenty-five other Jayhawkers were there. The gang's leader, a man named Chandler, stepped forward to explain his plan. "Secretly visit certain [Missouri] farms and collect all the horses possible," he instructed. "Bring them back [here], by dawn."

Under a waning but still bright moon, the men broke into groups of two or three. Then, traveling down deserted roads, they crept through fields and into barns and corrals. They chose, admitted Will, only the best horses. Slipping rope halters over the animals' heads, the men furtively led them away.

By dawn, the gang had stolen more than fifty mounts. Dividing the loot—each man got two horses—they struck out separately for the Kansas border.

"This action may look like horse-stealing, and some people might not hesitate to call it by that name," Will later wrote, "but Chandler plausibly maintained that we were only getting back our own . . . and as the government was waging war against the South, it was perfectly square and honest . . . So we didn't let our consciences trouble us very much."

Selling his two horses, Will returned to the Chandler gang. All summer long he and his fellow thieves galloped across the border to raid their Missouri neighbors. Jayhawking, Will discovered, was a lucrative business.

That is, until Mary Cody learned of his activities. "It [is] neither honorable nor right," she scolded. She demanded he quit.

Will reluctantly agreed. But just months later, he joined up with the Red Legged Scouts, or Red Legs, so called because of the red cloth they wrapped around their legs to distinguish themselves. The group did not belong to any military organization. Instead, it was an independent operation that claimed its purpose was to defend Kansas. But the truth, observed one Kansan, was that the Red Legs were "stealing themselves rich . . . and giving respectability to robbery when committed on anyone they declare disloyal." The Red Legs soon gained the reputation of being worse thieves and murderers than the Jayhawkers.

The Red Legs came and went as they wished. Without pay, they made their money by selling their victims' property—horses, guns, farm tools, silverware and china, even coats and bonnets, anything they could lay their hands on. They auctioned their ill-gotten goods openly on the streets of Leavenworth. They knew they had nothing to fear. No lawman dared stop them. Recalled Will, "In Leavenworth we . . . 'ran things' to suit ourselves."

By the spring of 1862 the Red Legs were out of control. They burned homes and robbed Unionists and Confederates alike.

Did Will join in these atrocities? He did confess to having "many a lively skirmish" with Missourians. But did he steal their property? Did he torch their homes?

We have some clues. In 1866—a year after the Civil War ended—Will was traveling aboard a Missouri River steamboat when he noticed some passengers glaring at him, pointing and whispering. "They say you are one of the Kansas jay-hawkers, and one of [the] house-burners," explained another person on board.

Will admitted he'd taken part in the guerrilla wars. "Perhaps these people know who I am," he said.

Did they? In his late teens during the war, Will would have stood out—handsome and already taller than most men. If he had been seen during the raids, he would not have been easily forgotten.

Will may or may not have participated in pillaging and house burning, but he certainly rode with men who did. And he made money as a member of the Red Legs. "The [cash] that Willie brought home and gave to Mother," Julia later recalled, "was a great help."

Will stayed with the Red Legs the entire summer of 1862. But he made only short trips with them the following fall and winter. That's because Mary Cody had grown so weak with tuberculosis she could no longer sit up on her own. Will often sat at her bedside, gently spooning broth into her mouth or dabbing her feverish forehead with a wet cloth. He promised not to stray too far from home.

But Julia knew she couldn't count on him to stay. "What do you think I better do?" she asked Will one night. Their mother wouldn't live much longer, and then Julia would be alone with three young girls and the seven-year-old Charlie.

Will thought a moment. "It seems like you better get married."

Julia agreed. She rattled off a list of possible husbands.

"No," Will said again and again, shaking his head at every name. "You do not want him."

Finally, Julia hit on Al Goodman, who was renting a farm just across the road.

Will banged his fist on the table. "Sister, he is the one for you to take!"

So Julia invited Al to supper. Sitting him down in front of a plate of fried chicken, she said, "Let's talk business not love, for my marrying [is] a business proposition."

Al agreed. Just days later, on December 22, 1862, the couple married. Julia's new husband immediately took over the farm chores. "It did seem so nice for me not to have to go out and get wood and do the milking," she admitted.

Will thought it nice, too. With another man looking after his family, he was free to return to the Red Legs, sometimes for weeks at a time, and enjoy the raiders' success. "I had money in my pocket," said Will. "I was able to [buy] an abundant supply of provisions for my family."

Almost a year after Julia's wedding, Will was out on a raiding trip when he received an urgent message from Julia: Mary Cody was dying.

Racing back to Salt Creek, Will arrived to find his mother barely alive, her body so pale and thin it seemed as if "her flesh had been refined away."

Mary beckoned her son to her bedside. Between rattling breaths, she reminded him of the fortune-teller's prediction so many years ago. His name *would* be famous the world over, she told him, but "only the names of them that are upright, brave . . . and true can be honorably known."

Will knew she was referring to his Red Leg activity. And he felt ashamed. "She never complained for herself," recalled Will, "her only thoughts being for her children . . . and setting them on a straight road [for] life." Holding her hand throughout that long night, he vowed to always be an honest man.

The sun was just rising on November 22, 1863, when Will kissed his mother for the last time. "Thus passed away . . . a noble, brave, good and loyal woman," said Will. "That I loved her above all other persons, no one . . . can for a moment doubt."

The next morning the family made the cold trip to Pilot Knob Cemetery. There they laid Mary's simple pine coffin in a muddy grave beside her husband's. "United in death as they had been in life," remarked Will's younger sister Helen. Somberly, the family made their way back home.

But at a fork in the road, Will leaped from the wagon. "I can't go home when I know Mother is no longer there," he cried. On foot, he headed to Leavenworth. He promised he'd only be gone overnight.

Instead, he stayed for two months. Despondent and guilt-ridden, he became "a very hard case," he later admitted. He drank and gambled and hung around with unsavory characters. It was, he said, "a dissolute and reckless life."

Then one February morning in 1864, Will awoke "after having been under the influence of bad whiskey" to discover he'd joined the Union Army. He was now a soldier in the Seventh Kansas Volunteer Cavalry! "I did not remember how or when I had enlisted, but I saw I was in for it, and that it would not do for me to [try] to back out." Eighteen-year-old Will Cody was headed for the battlefield.

PRIVATE CODY

We know very little about the one year, seven months, and ten days Will served with the Seventh Kansas. His regiment fought mostly in Mississippi and Missouri. It saw fierce combat at the Battle of Tupelo, where the Union Army— short of ammunition and rations—still managed to give Confederate forces a pounding. Later, the Seventh Kansas was sent north to defend St. Louis from a threatened Confederate invasion.

Private William F. Cody of the Seventh Kansas Cavalry. Taken in 1864 or 1865, the original image (a tintype) is locket-sized.

Years later in his autobiography, Will claimed he acted as a scout and spy for his regiment, riding ahead disguised as a Confederate soldier to gather information on the strength and location of enemy troops. His service record, however, tells a different story. It states that Will did not achieve any rank higher than private. And in January 1865 he was ordered to serve as a hospital orderly—hardly the type of posting that would have been given to the regiment's daring scout.

In January 1865, four months before the war ended, the army ordered Will to St. Louis to serve as a messenger for the Freedman's Bureau, a government agency formed to aid newly freed slaves. St. Louis—with its fancy hotels, public gardens, and streetcar-crowded avenues—was the biggest city Will had ever seen. He counted on having "a jolly good time."

What he didn't count on was Lulu.

A reenactment of a buffalo hunt (c. 1905). Bill is firing blanks at the calm-looking buffalo.

ACT FOUR

Becoming Buffalo Bill
Or
"Buffalo Hunt as It Was in the Far West of America—Buffalo Bill and Indians, the Last of the Only Known Native Herds."

—Buffalo Bill's Wild West Program, 1894

A Scene from the Wild West

A dozen placid buffalo cluster around a wooden trough painted to look like a prairie watering hole. But none of the animals drink. Instead, they graze on the armfuls of hay that have been thrown onto the showground. Their bearded chins go up and down. Their stump tails swat at the occasional fly.

Suddenly, Buffalo Bill's wild yell cuts through the silence. He gallops into the scene, followed by a group of Lakota men. Pop-pop-pop goes his Winchester rifle as it fires blanks at the animals. The Lakota fire as well.

The sound gets the tiny herd moving, but just barely. The buffalo canter solemnly around the track. They are not afraid. Regardless of the pretend hunters with their pounding hooves and noisy guns, the buffalo refuse to behave as if this is a real chase. They refuse to stampede to safety.

And yet the audience is not disappointed. They know the show arena is one of the few remaining places where buffalo can be found. Once, millions of *the animals had blanketed the plains; now barely more than a thousand remain. Showgoers feel lucky just to see this almost-extinct piece of American history. The buffalo—like the western frontier itself—is disappearing rapidly. Soon it will all be just memories—memories reenacted by Buffalo Bill's Wild West.*

The buffalo canter around the showground once, twice, three times, Bill and the other men shouting and whirling around them. Then a gate to one side of the arena is opened, and the animals agreeably trot through. The men lower their rifles and gallop into the wings. And Buffalo Bill brings his horse to a stop. He turns to the audience and raises his hand in the air—a greeting from the man who has long had the reputation of "Champion Buffalo Hunter of the Plains."

LULU

One evening early in 1865, twenty-two-year-old Louisa Frederici sat before the parlor's grate fire, reading a romance novel. Educated in a St. Louis convent, Louisa had recently returned to live with her parents in their fine two-story house in the city's French Quarter. Her father, a successful merchant, provided well for his family, and Lulu, as her family called her, was used to nice things like carriages and lace-trimmed dresses. Now, as she turned the pages, the sound of her sister dressing for the evening filtered downstairs. Their cousin William McDonald and his friend were expected for dinner. What was the friend's name? Lulu couldn't remember.

In the grate, the fire crackled.

Lulu's eyes grew heavy. Her head nodded. Her book dropped to her lap.

Then the chair was ripped out from under her.

A man laughed.

Scrambling to her feet, Lulu whirled furiously and lashed out.

"William McDonald," she cried as her hand made contact with her tormentor's face, "if you ever do that again, I'll—"

She stopped. The man rubbing his chin was *not* her cousin.

McDonald could barely contain his laughter. "Louisa," he said, "allow me to present Private William Frederick Cody of the United States Army."

Recalled Lulu, "My face was burning, and . . . I would have given anything to have pulled out . . . every hair on the head of my rollicking cousin."

Will Cody grinned. "I believe Miss Frederici and I have met before."

"Where?" asked Lulu.

Louisa (Lulu) Frederici—with her fashionable gowns and dark, expressive eyes—was a far cry from the women Will had known on the frontier. This photograph (c. 1870) was taken just a few years after their marriage.

"In battle," joked Will.

At that, both men howled with laughter.

Lulu flounced from the room. But not before noticing that Will Cody was "clean shaven . . . graceful, lithe, smooth in his movements," she later wrote. "He was quite the most wonderful man I had ever known, and I almost bit my tongue to keep from telling him so."

Will admired Lulu, too. "Her lovely face, her gentle disposition and her graceful manners won my admiration . . . ," he wrote. "I was not slow in declaring my sentiments to her."

He came alone to the Frederici house a few days later. Sitting with Lulu on the front porch, he held her spellbound with tales of his western adventures. By the time he left, she had fallen in love.

"I had been [educated] in a convent," she later explained. "My range of vision had not been large, my scope of reading had always been toward the romantic and adventurous [so] it felt natural that I should become fascinated by a man who had lived so eventful a life."

As for Will, he'd never known such a refined, well-educated woman. When he was mustered out of the army just weeks later, he left St. Louis with two things: a photograph of Lulu and her promise to marry him soon. "I considered myself one of the happiest of men," said Will.

But almost a year slipped by before the two finally tied the knot. Will, close to penniless, needed to earn some money before he took a wife. So he went back to Kansas, where he herded horses and drove a stagecoach. Finally, with a little money in his pocket, he returned to St. Louis. In front of the same parlor grate where they'd met, the couple exchanged vows in March 1866. The groom had just turned twenty; the bride was twenty-three.

An hour after the ceremony, the couple boarded a steamboat bound for Leavenworth. At first, Lulu found it all an adventure. She had never been outside St. Louis and everything was brand-new. The journey was, she thought, like something from one of her novels, "an explorer's trip on some unnavigated river."

By their third day together, though, Will noticed his bride "felt grieved." He couldn't understand her sudden sulkiness and tears. Little did he know that Lulu was already regretting her marriage decision. "I began to realize that I had said good-by to civilization," she later admitted, "that the comforts and safety of St. Louis might be a thing of the past forever. I knew now that I was going into a strange land where men often killed for the love of killing, where saloons and fights were common, where the life was coarse and rough and crude . . . I cringed at the thought of what was before me." Lulu was not cut out for the pioneer life.

And Will was not cut out for domesticity. Settling his bride into the Cody homestead on Salt Creek, he turned the place into a hotel called the Golden Rule House. "People generally said I made a good land-lord, and knew how to run a hotel," he recalled, "but it proved too tame employment for me, and again I sighed for the freedom of the plains." After just six months of marriage, he left Lulu behind and headed west.

Lulu longed to return to her parents' home in St. Louis. But she was pregnant. Worried the long trip might injure the baby, she stayed on at Salt Creek. There on December 16, 1866, she gave birth to their first daughter. She immediately telegraphed the news to Will. Days later, she heard his booming voice.

"What are we going to name it?" asked Will, pulling back the blanket and staring at the newborn.

According to Lulu, she suggested he choose the name.

But Will replied, "Me? The only thing I ever named was a horse and none of those names [would] do, would they?"

Lulu agreed they wouldn't.

"I've rather thought of the name Arta," said Lulu.

"Pretty name," said Will. He looked at the baby. "'Lo, Arta!"

But even the birth of his daughter could not keep Will home. Less than a week later, he galloped away. There was always something happening in the West, he explained to his wife, and he intended to be part of it.

Bitterly, Lulu said goodbye to Will. Then, packing up her new daughter, she returned to her parents' house in St. Louis.

"LOOKING AROUND FOR ANYTHING"

Will rode out to the end of the line. That is, he traveled to where the railroad tracks stopped in western Kansas. At that time, the Kansas Pacific Railway was being built across the Great Plains, and swarms of men followed, looking for work. This led to makeshift towns that sprang up along the ever-expanding route. The towns were, recalled one visitor, little more than "beer houses, whisky shops, gambling houses [and] dance houses" where men got drunk, played cards and shell games, and "chronicled the nightly murders in the town."

The end of the line, or Ellsworth, Kansas, where Will headed in 1867, the same year this photograph was taken. Teeming with railroad workers, buffalo hunters, gamblers, and outlaws, Ellsworth gained a reputation for being the wickedest town in the state.

It was here that Will scrabbled to make a living. "[I was] railroading and trading and hunting," he said. "I went out to make money, and I was just looking around for anything that would come along."

That winter he lived in a dugout, much like the one he and Dave Harrington had built near Prairie Dog Creek back in 1859. Sharing this dark, cramped space with two other men, he worked at odd jobs. For a short time he pushed a wheelbarrow for the Kansas Pacific. Later he hauled supplies for a friend who was setting up a dry-goods store. He even briefly sold whiskey on the street. Unfortunately, he didn't have the necessary license to sell liquor. None of these jobs was the way Will had imagined making his fortune.

In the summer of 1867, he teamed up with a man named William Rose. Rose suggested they found a town, and Will jumped at the chance. Choosing several acres along the west side of Big Creek (where they expected the railroad to cross), they surveyed the land and staked it off into plots. Their plan was to sell the plots for fifty dollars apiece. That's all it took to get a town started back then. Pooling the little money they had, the two men bought some supplies and built a crude store with a wooden frame and a tent roof. Believing in the town's future greatness, Will named it Rome.

And people came. "In less than one month we had two hundred frame, log houses, three or four stores, several saloons and one good hotel," recalled Will. Convinced he had "the world by the tail" and would soon become a millionaire, he sent for Lulu and Arta. He not only had a home, he bragged to her, but he was worth $250,000. (He was—on paper. But since no one had yet paid for the land he and Rose had staked out, he had nothing in his pocket.)

Thrilled to think that her husband had finally become the middle-class businessman she longed for, Lulu met Will at the end of the tracks.

The exodus of Rome as depicted in Cody's 1879 autobiography.

But when she stepped off the train, she realized her mistake. "I dropped my arms aghast," she recalled. Rome was nothing but shacks and tents. Where was her comfortable house? It turned out to be the back of the store. Lulu detested every minute of it—the cramped single room, the leaky canvas roof. From the saloon next door came the shouts and laughter of drunken railroad workers. Fights often broke out, waking the baby.

One afternoon, just months after the town's establishment, a well-dressed man stopped in at the store. Introducing himself to Will as Dr. W. E. Webb, he said, "You've got a flourishing little town here. Wouldn't you like to have [another] partner?"

"No thank you," Will quickly replied. "We have too good a thing here to whack up with anybody [else]."

Dr. Webb then explained that he was the agent for the Kansas Pacific Railway and it was his job to establish towns along the line. The railroad expected to make money by selling land and town lots. Since Cody and Rose refused to share with the railroad, Dr. Webb had no choice but to start another town nearby.

"Start your town if you want to," snapped Will.

That's exactly what Webb did. The very next day he staked out a new settlement just one mile east of Rome. Calling it Hays City, he let it be known that his town was where the train would stop. He even offered to move everyone from Rome to Hays City for free.

"A ruinous stampede from our place was the result," recalled Will.

"People . . . began pulling down their buildings and moving them over . . . and in less than three days our once flourishing city had dwindled down to the little store which Rose and I had built."

As they watched the stream of wagons rolling away, Lulu looked "rather blue," remembered Will.

"Where's the $250,000 that you are worth?" she cried.

"I told her that I expected it had gone off with the town," said Will. "That I was busted."

In a furious huff, Lulu took the baby and went right back to St. Louis.

And Will went looking for another job.

The job he found was buffalo hunting.

"Buffalo Bill, Buffalo Bill, Never Missed and Never Will"

At this time, Will owned a prize stallion named Brigham that he'd bought months earlier from a Ute man. The horse, he said, "was the fleetest steed I ever owned." It had also been trained to chase down buffalo so that its rider could easily shoot them.

It was on Brigham that Will first rode out to the prairie to hunt buffalo. Spotting a herd, the two galloped up on it from behind. Riding in close, Will raised his favorite hunting gun, a .50-caliber Springfield rifle he called Lucretia Borgia, to his shoulder. He fired, killing the buffalo in one shot. Brigham then carried him alongside the next animal, and Will dropped it with his next shot. "As soon as one buffalo would fall, Brigham would take me so close to the next that I could almost touch it with my gun," explained Will. Before long, "there were few men who . . . could kill more buffalo on a hunt than [I could]," he bragged. Butchering the animals on the spot, he sold the meat at nearby Fort Hays.

Nowadays, many people think of buffalo hunters as careless destroyers of wildlife. But in Will's day settlers in the American West saw hunting buffalo as a respectable job. That's because they welcomed the eradication of the buffalo. They believed that if the herd vanished, so, too, would the Plains tribes. After all, the tribes depended on the animal for their survival; the buffalo was the lifeblood of their culture. The reasoning went that if the animals were eliminated, Native people would have no choice but to settle down on reservations and become wards of the U.S. government. And the "Indian problem," as it was often called, would be solved.

In October 1867, the Kansas Pacific Railway advertised for a buffalo hunter. The railroad's twelve hundred tracklayers had now reached deep into buffalo country and needed to be fed. Kansas Pacific officials were looking for someone who could provide twelve buffalo a day. Will offered his services and was immediately hired.

A woodcut from his 1879 autobiography shows Will mounted on Brigham and demonstrating his special buffalo-hunting technique.

Every morning, mounted on Brigham, Will rode away from the safety of the railroad camp. Alone except for the butcher who followed behind in a mule-pulled wagon, Will scoured the horizon for signs of both buffalo and American Indians. In case of an attack, he'd prearranged a signal with the cavalry troops stationed along the railroad tracks—a brushfire, the smoke from which would be visible for miles around. As for buffalo, sometimes Will traveled ten miles or more before spotting a herd. Then he and Brigham got to work, chasing and shooting.

"During my engagement as a hunter for the company [from October 1867 to May 1868] I killed 4,280 buffalo," boasted Will, "and I had many exciting adventures, as well as hair-breadth escapes."

According to Will, one of those escapes took place on an April day in 1868. He and a butcher named Scotty had already loaded up the wagon with the day's meat when thirty American Indians thundered out of a nearby ravine. In a flash, the hunters piled up the buffalo hams to form a barricade. Then Will lit the signal brushfire to the windward side of the wagon. Would the cavalry see the smoke in time? He hunkered down next to Scotty behind the mountain of meat. With the extra rifles and ammunition they always carried, the men fended off the attack.

For almost an hour, the two sides blazed away at each other. At last, Will and Scotty saw the cavalry charging toward them across the prairie. Their attackers saw them, too. Wheeling their horses, they rode away. And Will and Scotty reloaded the wagon. "Later, we pulled into camp with our load of meat which was found to be all right, except that it had a few bullets and arrows sticking in it," remembered Will.

Not surprisingly, the railroad workers soon tired of their steady diet of bison meat. "Here comes this old Bill with more buffalo," they grumbled whenever they saw his wagon pull into camp. Finally, said Will, "they connected the names Buffalo and Bill together, and that is where the foundation was laid to the name 'Buffalo Bill.'"

Around the same time, the workmen made up a jingle about Will. It became so popular that it was reprinted in the local newspaper:

> Buffalo Bill, Buffalo Bill,
> Never missed and never will;
> Always aims and shoots to kill
> And the company pays his buffalo bill.

It was hardly an original nickname. There were dozens of Buffalo Bills out west—William J. "Buffalo Bill" Wilson, who was hanged for murder in New Mexico; "Buffalo Billy" Brooks, a sheriff in Dodge City, Kansas; South Dakota rancher William C. Tomlins, who was known as the "Buffalo Bill of the Black Hills," to name just a few.

And then there was William "Buffalo Bill" Comstock, guide and interpreter at nearby Fort Wallace in Kansas. According to Will, Comstock was infuriated by Will's use of the nickname and proposed a contest. The winner not only would earn the right to use the name "Buffalo Bill" but would win the title of "Champion Buffalo Hunter of the Plains" as well.

"CHAMPION BUFFALO HUNTER OF THE PLAINS"

As Will tells it, the contest was advertised all across Kansas and as far away as St. Louis. One morning, a surprised Lulu came upon a glaring poster in a downtown shop window. It read: "Buffalo shooting match for . . . the championship of the world between Billy Comstock, the famous scout, and W. F. Cody, famous buffalo hunter for the Kansas Pacific Railway." What was her husband up to now? She marched down to the train station to buy a ticket.

She wasn't the only one. "A large crowd witnessed . . . the [contest]," Will later claimed. "An excursion party, mostly from St. Louis, consisting of about a hundred gentlemen and ladies, came on a special train to view the sport." Lulu and baby Arta were among them.

The hunt, claimed Will, was expected to last from eight in the morning until four in the afternoon. Riding into the herd at the same time, each competitor would try to kill as many buffalo as he could. To eliminate cheating, a scorekeeper would trail behind them.

As he squinted into the morning sunlight waiting for the starting gun to fire, Will felt confident. Not only was he mounted on "the best buffalo horse that ever made a track," but he also carried "my favorite old Lucretia." He figured Comstock didn't stand a chance.

Bang! The starting gun fired.

"Comstock and I dashed into the herd," recalled Will. "The buffalo separated; Comstock took the left bunch and I took the right. My great forte in killing buffaloes from horseback was to get them circling . . . round and round. On this morning [they] were very accommodating and I soon had them running in a beautiful circle, when I dropped them thick and fast, until I had killed thirty-eight . . . Comstock began shooting at the rear of the herd, which he was chasing and they kept straight on. He . . . killed twenty-three."

After this first run, the contestants took a break and the St. Louis spectators poured a round of champagne. It "proved a good drink on a Kansas prairie," remembered Will. Revived, the two men tore off on their second run. This time Will killed eighteen buffalo, Comstock fourteen.

Lunchtime brought another break and even more champagne. The bubbles must have gone straight to Will's head. "I thought I could afford to give an extra exhibition of my skill," he bragged. Yanking saddle and bridle off Brigham, he charged bareback into the herd.

The ladies gasped at his daring.

The gentlemen cheered.

And Will handily downed twelve more buffalo.

It was the thirteenth that caused problems.

Some of the St. Louis folks had ridden down in a wagon for a better view of the slaughter. Showing off, Will skillfully drove the herd near them, just to give the ladies a thrill. Unexpectedly, one of the buffalo broke away and charged toward them.

Clutching one another, the ladies shrieked with fear.

And Will thundered to the rescue. In a split second he aimed and fired. The animal "dropped dead in its tracks" just feet from the spectator-packed wagon. It was Will's thirteenth buffalo, and it brought the contest's final tally to Cody, sixty nine; Comstock, forty-six.

"Thereupon, the referees declared me the winner of the match," Bill bragged, "as well as champion buffalo hunter of the plains."

More important, he had won the right to the contested nickname "Buffalo Bill." Said Will—now Buffalo Bill—proudly, "Of this [name], which has stuck to me through life, I have never been ashamed."

✦ PANNING FOR THE TRUTH ✦
WINNING THE NAME "BUFFALO BILL"

Buffalo-hunting competitions *were* common on the frontier. Railroads often advertised them in hopes would-be tourists would hop a train and head west. It worked. "Persons from the east are stopping off here every day, hoping to get a chance to witness . . . a buffalo hunt," reported one Topeka journalist.

But did tourists really board a train bound for the Cody-Comstock contest? It appears doubtful. No one has ever learned the exact date or location of the event. Will—or now Bill—never gave these details in his autobiography, and no poster, newspaper article, or advertisement has ever surfaced.

This is especially curious, considering Bill claimed the event was "pretty well advertised and noised about." More perplexing is the lack of eyewitness accounts. If a hundred spectators really did travel to Kansas to watch such a contest, surely someone would have mentioned it in some written document. But no memoir, diary entry, or letter has ever turned up. Neither has a single railroad document. Instead, the historical record remains suspiciously silent.

And then there is William Comstock himself. In 1868—the year Bill Cody claims the contest took place—Comstock was wanted for murder. It's doubtful a man running from the law would have appeared at such a well-advertised, well-attended event. And if he did, it's strange that he never made mention of the contest.

What to make of it all?

Some historians argue that the contest simply never happened. They contend that, to bolster his own reputation as a sharpshooting buffalo hunter, Bill made up the story after Comstock's death (so Comstock couldn't deny it). Others maintain that the story is true but exaggerated. Yes, the match happened, they claim; it just didn't happen the way Bill said it did. Instead of the championship of the world, remarked one historian, it was more like a "pick-up game of sand-lot baseball gotten up . . . on the spur of the moment by the neighborhood fellows."

STORMY DAYS WITH LULU

Whether they came with the special excursion party or traveled on their own, Lulu and eighteen-month-old Arta returned to Kansas in

June 1868. Bill rented two small rooms for them in a boardinghouse in Leavenworth, close enough that he could occasionally visit from the railroad camp. He hoped to mend his marriage.

But Lulu had lost faith in her husband. To her mind, going from town founder to buffalo hunter was a step backward. So what if he was earning steady money? His latest occupation embarrassed her. "She made little of my efforts to succeed in life," Bill remembered. "[She said] I was a failure."

One night the couple had a terrible fight. About what, no one knows. When Bill finally left the boardinghouse, he believed his marriage was over. "I didn't think that we would ever have another meeting," he recalled. "We had kind o' mutually agreed that we were not suited to each other; she was as glad to go back to [St. Louis] as I was to go to the plains."

As he rode off alone, Bill pondered his future. He knew his time as a buffalo hunter had come to an end. The railroad tracks had pushed as far as Sheridan, Kansas, and construction was being abandoned temporarily. So what to do next?

"At this time there was a general Indian war raging all along the western borders," said Bill. "As such, scouts and guides were in great demand."

He spurred his stallion Brigham westward.

GALLOPING INTO A WAR ZONE

The conflict between Native people and settlers had raged for centuries, long before Bill got involved. Only thirty years earlier, the federal government had established what it called the Permanent Indian Frontier. Encompassing a vast swath of acreage west of the Mississippi River, it was meant to separate Native people from white settlers. Government officials pressured tribes living in the east to trade their ancestral homeland for territory in the Permanent Indian Frontier. In return they promised to "forever secure and guarantee" those lands to the tribes for future generations. While many eastern tribes resisted, by 1840 almost all of them had been brutally forced out of their native lands. The federal government hoped this banishment to a separate and reserved area would end the conflict between American Indians and settlers.

But with the discovery of gold in California in 1848, settlers began streaming across the Permanent Indian Frontier. The horses, oxen, and wagon wheels made deep ruts in tribal land. The animals consumed all the grass and the people used up all the wood for miles on either side of their trails, leaving almost nothing for Native people's game animals to eat. When they did come upon a herd of buffalo, settlers wastefully killed them, taking only the best meat and leaving the rest of the carcasses to rot in the sun.

Not surprisingly, American Indians' resentment built. This was their land. They had a treaty with the United States government that said so. Tensions heightened. There was sporadic fighting.

But the federal government did little to protect American Indian rights. Instead, it caved in to pressure from settlers. Abandoning the idea of the Permanent Indian Frontier, it instituted a new policy. By the 1850s, government officials had begun forcing tribes—through economic sanctions and military threat—to once again sign treaties ceding their land. This time tribes received small, isolated reservations with poor soil and little game. How could they survive? The government's promise to provide food and supplies meant nothing. More often than not, the provisions failed to arrive.

Trapped on these reservations—without game to hunt and with no way of growing crops in the arid climate—American Indians grew desperate. Some were reduced to begging for food from settlers. Others felt they had no choice but to move back to their former hunting grounds. Chief Black Kettle's band of Cheyenne did just that in 1864.

It was the spark that would ignite a powder keg.

A regiment of seven hundred volunteers led by a pistol-packing Methodist preacher named John Chivington attacked the Cheyenne. No matter that Chief Black Kettle had, over the years, made repeated attempts to secure an honorable peace with settlers. He'd even spoken with the local military commander at Fort Weld just hours before the attack. The commander led Black Kettle to believe that his people would be protected by the U.S. Army if they made camp on the shores of Sand Creek, southeast of Denver, Colorado.

The commander lied.

At dawn on November 29, 1864, Chivington and his men—many of them drunk—approached Black Kettle's sleeping camp. "Kill and scalp all, big and little," cried Chivington.

Black Kettle stood before his lodge waving an American flag. He called out to his people not to be frightened. Their camp was under the protection of the U.S. government, he shouted. There was no danger. Men, women, and children huddled beneath the Stars and Stripes. Someone else raised a white flag, the symbol of surrender.

Chivington's men paid no attention. They fired into the lodges. Recalled one member of the regiment, "We, of course, took no prisoners."

When the massacre ended, four hundred Cheyenne—most of them women and children—lay murdered. Chivington's men scalped and mutilated many of the dead. Later they exhibited their gruesome souvenirs to cheering crowds in Denver.

Word of the horror at Sand Creek swept through other tribal communities. They agreed: the settlers must be met with force. From western Kansas to Utah, bands of Sioux, Arapaho, and Cheyenne burned stagecoaches and tore down telegraph wires. They shot railroad workers and, in one instance, pulled up the tracks, derailing a train. They seized supply wagons, drove off stock, burned cabins, and killed settlers.

The government responded by sending several hundred troops west. Their orders were clear: drive the Cheyenne from Kansas and Nebraska. For four frustrating months in 1866, the troops bumbled across the prairie. In that time they managed to find and kill just two Cheyenne men. Meanwhile, Cheyenne warriors killed more than two hundred settlers.

Back in Washington, officials began questioning their policy. It seemed foolhardy to spend so much money chasing after American Indians without ever catching them. Perhaps a less harsh approach to the problem would work. So, in 1867, Congress authorized a peace delegation to head west.

Once again treaties were signed. Once again American Indians agreed to go to specified reservations. But few made any move toward the designated areas, and the army didn't press.

Then in the summer of 1868, officers at Fort Larned, in central Kansas, refused to give rifles and ammunition to a band of Cheyenne as promised under terms of the new treaty. Angry at being cheated once again, the Cheyenne began raiding settlers along the Saline and Solomon Rivers. Once more, they burned, raided, and killed.

The federal government turned to General Philip Sheridan. A ruthless soldier, Sheridan was given command of all troops in Kansas, Oklahoma, Colorado, and New Mexico. He immediately devised a plan to fight a winter war when American Indian ponies were weak and warriors stayed in their villages. He noted that "an Indian with a fat pony is very different from him with a starved one." Of course, a winter war meant attacking villages full of innocent bystanders. What about them? "If a village is attacked and women and children killed," said the coldhearted general, "the responsibility is not with the soldiers, but with the people whose crimes necessitated the attack."

In March 1868, Sheridan—eager to crush the Cheyenne—took up his new post at Fort Hays.

Six months later, he met Bill Cody.

BILL CODY: SCOUT

Scouting for the U.S. Army suited Bill. Not only did he earn seventy-five dollars a month, but unlike the enlisted men, he was free to come and go as he pleased. That's because scouts remained civilians who were paid by the job. Bill was not required to wear a uniform, take part in military drills, or sleep in the soldiers' barracks. Still, he often found himself alongside the troops as bullets whizzed overhead. Then—uniformed or not—he obeyed the commanding officer just like any soldier would. And he fought just as hard, too.

In the eight weeks he'd been at Fort Larned he had already found himself in two skin-of-the-teeth skirmishes. And he'd had a close call with a band of Kiowa who'd chased him for miles before he'd given them the slip. Daily, he risked his life, carrying dispatches from one post to another, riding alone ahead of troops in search of American Indians or a safe route. And Bill loved it. "It was interesting, and I may say, exciting," he said.

He also felt useful. Soldiers who came from the East knew almost nothing about the Great Plains. The long, treeless vistas looked like flat land. But in truth, the plains rolled and tilted. Beneath the knee-high grasses, streams cut through the unbroken prairie sod, creating unexpected gorges and gullies, as well as jagged, twisting canyons. Paths that looked straight changed direction subtly, leading inexperienced troops far off course. Without someone who knew the land, soldiers often got lost.

Cody's skills were extraordinary. Not only could he find his way across the deceptive grasslands, but he could tell at a glance if the black

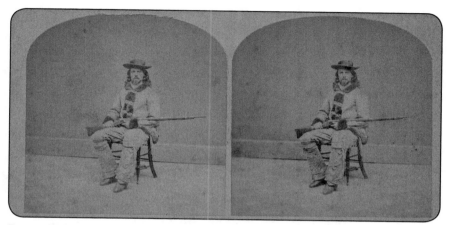

The scout Bill Cody, c. 1870, holding his legendary rifle "Lucretia Borgia." The picture is a stereoscope with a young Bill sitting in buckskin with a rifle across his lap.

dots on the horizon were buffalo or horses. He could forge ahead and clear a path for others, marking his trail by using a grass knot, or tussock, to show followers the way. He could even identify noises of all kinds and read a landscape for clues of a recent tribe's passing. Moreover, he could find food, water, and shelter in the most barren landscape. And he always knew the best places to set up camp. "His eyesight is better than a good field-glass," praised one commanding officer. "He is a perfect judge of distance. His trailing when following Indians or looking for game is simply wonderful. He is a most extraordinary hunter."

Now he was about to prove his mettle as a messenger.

A DANGEROUS UNDERTAKING

Fort Larned crackled with tension. Word had just arrived that the Comanche and Kiowa were angry with settlers and preparing to fight. The fort's commander, Captain Daingerfield Parker, immediately placed double guards on duty. Then he called together his scouts. One of them had to ride to Fort Hays, some sixty-five miles away, and notify General Sheridan. Which of them would it be?

One by one, the scouts shook their heads. It was a fool's errand. A storm was coming up, and night was falling. Besides, a band of Kiowa had pitched camp near the road to Fort Hays. This meant the direct route was impossible. A rider would have to cross the hilly and treacherous countryside in the dark, a risky undertaking.

Bill stepped forward. "I'll go," he volunteered. "I have hunted on nearly every acre of ground between here and Fort Hays and I can almost [find] my way by the bones of the dead buffalo." He asked for just one thing—a good, fast horse.

At times like these Bill sorely missed Brigham. Months earlier, "having no suitable place to leave my faithful old buffalo hunter, and not wishing to kill him by scouting," he'd reluctantly sold the stallion. Now he rode the typical mount of a plains scout—a mule.

But a mule wouldn't do for this errand. Captain Parker ordered the fort's fastest horse brought up from the stable.

After filling a canteen with brandy and tucking Captain Parker's dispatches into his boot, Bill climbed into the saddle. The fort's gates clattered opened and the scout galloped into the night.

Keeping to a familiar path, he traveled at a steady pace until he came to a ravine near Walnut Creek. He knew the Kiowa camp was not far away. Picking his way quietly through a stand of trees, he skirted the camp—or so he thought. Suddenly, he found himself in the middle of a herd of ponies! The animals began to snort and whinny and paw the ground. A dog started to howl. Instantly, the darkness teemed with Kiowa, all racing for their mounts. A handful of the quickest men leaped onto their ponies and tore after the intruder.

Bill sped away. No matter the uneven ground or the darkness. He urged his horse on, over ridges and along creek bottoms. At last he came to a river. Horse and rider took it in a single leap. On the opposite bank, the men pulled their horses up. As the scout plunged into the night, they turned back for their camp.

Bill slowed and took a steadying gulp of brandy. Then—after checking his compass by the light of a burning match—he picked his way slowly, carefully, across the dark plain once more. "I was afraid of running into another band of Indians," he confessed. "[But all] I scared up [was] . . . coyotes or deer . . . With the exception of these slight alarms I got along all right." He trotted through the gates at Fort Hays just as the army bugler was playing reveille.

General Sheridan was still in bed when Bill strode in to deliver the dispatches. Even in his pajamas, the general looked tough as nails. His dark eyes scanned the dispatches before squinting at Bill. "I suppose you're tired after your journey," he said. "Come in and have some breakfast with me."

Bill declined the invitation. Climbing back into the saddle, he rode the five miles to Hays City to visit with some friends. When he returned to the fort a few hours later, he found the other scouts with their heads together, whispering.

General Sheridan, they told him, wanted an important message delivered to Fort Dodge, ninety-five miles away. He'd even offered a bonus of one hundred dollars to any scout who would make the trip. But all refused to go. American Indian warriors had killed the last three men who had tried to deliver dispatches over that route.

Once again, Bill stepped forward. "General . . . I'll carry your dispatches myself."

"I gratefully accepted his offer," Sheridan later recalled. "He mounted a fresh horse and hastened on his journey . . . At Dodge he took six hours' sleep and then continued on to his own post—Fort Larned, with more dispatches. [But] twelve hours later he was again in the saddle with more tidings for me at Fort Hays . . . Such an exhibition of endurance and courage [was] enough to convince me that his services would be extremely valuable."

The general promoted Bill to chief of scouts for the Fifth Cavalry. This meant that Sheridan would ask Bill's advice before hiring other scouts. It also meant he'd be hired for scouting jobs before anyone else.

Now the busiest scout in the territory, Bill accompanied the Fifth—under the command of Brevet Major General Eugene Carr—to forts all over Kansas. He fought often. In October 1868, he helped fend off a Cheyenne attack near Fort Wallace. And he faced off with Cheyenne, Sioux, and Arapaho warriors in a series of skirmishes around Beaver Creek.

In the late fall of that year, Cody and the Fifth moved to take part in Sheridan's "winter war." Pushing out from Fort Lyon in Colorado Territory, they scouted along the Canadian River in search of American Indian camps. Recorded General Carr, "We encountered hardships and exposure in terrific snowstorms [and] sleet." But they didn't see a single American Indian.

By February 1869, Cody and the Fifth headed back to Fort Lyon. But they were soon ordered to Fort McPherson in Nebraska.

A PLACE TO CALL HOME

Twenty-three-year-old Bill Cody first saw Fort McPherson on a balmy May day in 1869. He was impressed. Built on thirty-eight acres of dusty prairie, the place looked more like a small town than a frontier outpost. There were framed houses for officers' families and comfortable log barracks for enlisted men. Workshops—carpentry, saddlery, blacksmith—lined the west side of the parade ground. On the east side stood a barbershop, a post office, and two pool halls—one for the officers and one for the enlisted men. Regular soldiers even had a library complete with 38 books, while officers had their choice of 362 volumes. Above it all, from a pole placed in the center of the parade ground, fluttered the U.S. flag boasting thirty-seven stars, Nebraska being the thirty-seventh state.

From dawn to dusk, the fort bustled with activity. Wagon trains came and went. Columns of troops arrived and departed. Mail coaches and mounted couriers pounded into the fort. Because there was a railroad stop in the town of McPherson, just four miles away, all sorts of unexpected visitors arrived at the fort. Military brass, rich businessmen, politicians, and ordinary tourists appeared daily.

Dances were held on Friday nights, and folks came from far and wide to attend. The officers' ladies held tea parties and formed knitting circles. And every Saturday night, troops put on a performance in the fort's theater. The pride of the post, the theater had not only a stage and seating but dressing rooms as well.

Bill wasn't much interested in the dramatic readings or sewing circles. But he looked forward to those dances. What better way to get in good favor with the officers and their wives? He knew these were the people who could help him cross the divide between working-class and middle-class Americans. And Bill hankered to move beyond his frontier roots.

But those dances would have to wait. Just days after his arrival at the fort, a large party of Cheyenne led by Chief Tall Bull, along with three bands of Sioux and some Arapaho warriors, swept across northern Kansas, destroying homesteads and killing settlers. General Sheridan believed the warriors would turn north toward the Powder River country of Wyoming. He ordered the Fifth Cavalry to pursue them.

A TALE OF TALL BULL

On the afternoon of June 8, 1869, before their departure, the Fifth put on a full-dress review for the entire McPherson garrison and their families. As the nearly four hundred troops marched in formation across the parade ground, a military band struck up a tune. Flags waved. Sabers glinted. From the reviewing stand, General Carr saluted smartly.

Behind the troops came the 150 members of the Pawnee battalion. These men, under the very loose command of translator Major Frank North, had chosen to side with the U.S. Army in the war against other Native tribes, and were some of the best scouts in the military. For today's review, they had been given full-dress uniforms. But the men wore just bits and pieces of them. Some donned the regulation pants but no shirts. Others wore a shirt over a simple breechclout. Still others chose to wear just the heavy overcoat or the large black hat or the brass spurs without the boots. The Pawnee men, claimed Bill, who watched the review from the sidelines, "felt proud and elated."

So did Bill. At that moment, his love of pomp, parades, and military reviews was ignited. Time and again he would reenact this day for audiences of his Wild West show.

The next morning, just after reveille, the troops headed out. Mile after mile they rode, through swollen streams and up steep sandbanks, the summer sun blazing down on them. They found abandoned Cheyenne campsites but little else. Neither Bill nor the Pawnee scouts could pick up a trail. Exhaustion set in. It appeared the Fifth had reached its limit.

General Carr ordered one last effort. Choosing just the men whose horses were still strong, he set off at dawn on July 11 with 244 cavalry, 50 Pawnee scouts, Major Frank North and his brother Luther, and Bill. They carried enough rations for three days. If they did not find the Cheyenne by then, Carr decided, they would turn back.

"I was ordered to pick five or six of the best Pawnees to track the Indians," Bill recalled. Keeping ten miles ahead of the regiment, they scoured the tops of the hills for any sign of Tall Bull's camp. Around midmorning, the Pawnee scouts discovered footprints. A trail! Moving cautiously, they soon discovered a big camp tucked into a valley at White Butte. Leaving the Pawnee to keep watch, Bill rode back to the regiment with the news—the enemy was in sight.

That same afternoon, Carr's men attacked. Taken completely by surprise, the Cheyenne didn't have a chance to organize themselves or defend their families. Running in all directions, snatching at horses where they could, they raced for the safety of ravines and hills. "We went through the village shooting right and left at everything we saw," recalled Bill.

In the chaos, Chief Tall Bull grabbed a pony. Lifting one of his wives onto its back with him, he raced into a steep, narrow ravine. After making sure his wife was safe inside, he rode back to the ravine's opening.

That's when Bill claimed to have shot him. "I noticed an Indian who was riding . . . an extraordinary [horse], fleet as the wind," he said. Wanting the horse for himself, he crept to the mouth of the ravine and hid. "I waited there until Mr. Chief came riding by."

When he did, Bill fired.

Tall Bull tumbled from the horse.

And Bill climbed on. "Little did I think at the time that I had captured a horse . . . which was the fastest runner in the state of Nebraska."

✧ PANNING FOR THE TRUTH ✧
THE DEATH OF CHIEF TALL BULL

Bill's version of Tall Bull's death is certainly dramatic. But does it agree with other accounts of that event? Not at all.

In his own written report of the battle, General Carr

---

recalled an interview with one of the chief's wives. She claimed Tall Bull died while fighting on foot, because he no longer had a horse. Wrote Carr, "The wife begged [Tall Bull] to escape with her, but he shut his ears, killed his horse [as a sign he would not retreat], and she soon saw him killed fighting."

Her testimony agreed with Luther North's account. He, too, remembered seeing Tall Bull firing on foot from the mouth of a ravine. Later he would claim his brother Frank shot the chief.

Additionally, a painting made by a Cheyenne eyewitness after the fight showed Tall Bull on foot in a ravine. His killer, according to this record, was a Pawnee scout.

And the Pawnee? They claimed it was impossible to know who killed Tall Bull. That's because dozens of men were shooting at him as the chief stood at the mouth of a ravine.

Regardless of who killed Tall Bull, it was a devastating loss for the Cheyenne. With his leadership gone, resistance was broken and hostilities in Kansas began to lessen.

BUFFALO BILL, THE KING OF BORDER MEN

One sweltering July morning just days after his return to Fort Mc-Pherson, Bill noticed a stout middle-aged man sitting in the shade of a cottonwood tree. Even though the man wore a blue uniform, he hardly looked fit enough to be an army officer.

"Cody, allow me to introduce to you Colonel [Edward Zane Carroll] Judson, otherwise known as Ned Buntline," said one of the officers.

Bill recognized the second name. Ned Buntline was the author of many hugely popular dime novels. Cheaply made paperbacks that cost just ten cents apiece, dime novels were lurid, outlandish tales of adventure and melodrama. Buntline—who bragged he could write six of these novels a week and did produce more than four hundred of them during his long writing career—was both rich and famous. Now he'd come west in search of a hero to write about.

Buntline took in the man who stood before him. Tall, with long brown hair, Cody looked the part of a heroic westerner in his buckskin jacket. But did he have skills?

Later that same day, a detachment of the Fifth Cavalry headed out on a routine expedition. Buntline went with them. He watched with interest as Bill uncovered an American Indian trail. The troops followed it for a few miles. But the commanding officer soon ordered their return to the fort. Horses wheeled—all except Bill's. He was headed toward Fort Sedgwick in Colorado. Buntline asked to tag along. "During this short [ride]," recalled Bill, "[he] asked me a great many questions." Always a good storyteller, Bill regaled Buntline with tales of his frontier adventures—harrowing fights, exciting buffalo hunts, and danger-fraught wagon train crossings.

Buntline had found his hero. By the time he returned to New York City, his head was stuffed with blood-and-thunder stories. Just four months later, the serialized story "Buffalo Bill, the King of Border Men" appeared in a New York newspaper. Advertised as the "wildest and truest story" Buntline had ever written, it was pure fiction.

In Buntline's tale, Buffalo Bill—along with gunslinger and lawman Wild Bill Hickok—rescues his mother and sisters from a gang of murderous renegades. Bill's character is established as sort of a western action hero. Reads one passage: "On through the mass dashed Buffalo Bill, revolver in each hand, and shot after shot, in the face of his opponents, dropped a man at every fire . . . Every shot had been fired from his revolver, but now his great knife-blade flashed in the air and came sweeping down here and there, as he saw foes to strike." At story's end, as Bill rides off into the sunset, Buntline writes, "Buffalo Bill is just as good as was ever made . . . There isn't a bit of white in his liver, nor black in his heart."

Almost overnight, Buffalo Bill became one of the best-known figures of the Wild West. The story's timing was perfect. Readers back east were looking for a white western hero. Newspapers vividly reported the campaigns against the American Indian, and the building of both the transcontinental railroad and the telegraph made the frontier feel close. Longing for a western hero, easterners quickly fell under Buffalo Bill's spell. They bought up Buntline's story and begged for more.

They got it. "Buffalo Bill, the King of Border Men" was just the first of seventeen hundred stories written about Cody during his lifetime. Although Ned Buntline is often mistakenly credited with authoring most or all of them, in truth he wrote just three more. Bill's advance man and publicist, Prentiss Ingraham, would later write the majority.

PLAYING A JOKE ON MCCARTHY

The publication of Ned Buntline's story took Bill by surprise. He hadn't known Buntline was writing it. Still, it pleased and flattered him. Now if only he could figure out a way to capitalize on his celebrity. He was still scouting for seventy-five dollars a month. But things had grown more peaceful on the Great Plains, and his skills weren't needed as often. So what next? He decided to offer his services to the trainloads of wealthy easterners who arrived at McPherson Station looking for a bit of western excitement. He figured they'd pay top dollar to have Buffalo Bill, the King of Border Men, as their hunting guide.

He was right. In the first months of 1870, Bill guided a British earl searching for elk and a Yale University scientist searching for dinosaur bones. He guided congressmen and railroad magnates and foreign dignitaries. A steady stream of rich hunters kept him busy. And with each party he led, he grew more experienced at providing his "sports," as he called them, with a western experience.

He came to understand that easterners expected the West to look like the one they saw in paintings and read about in newspapers and dime novels. That meant they wanted not only to shoot at herds of buffalo but to encounter Native people, too. Accounts of the Plains Wars had left them captivated by the ways of American Indians. And so Bill hired the Pawnee scouts to ride along on hunting expeditions or perform ceremonial dances around the campfire.

Once he even convinced a handful of them to stage an attack. Shouting and firing their rifles into the air, the Pawnee scouts, pretending to be raiders, raced down a creek bed toward Bill and his sport, a rich New York banker identified only as Mr. McCarthy.

Playing his part, Bill shouted, "Should we dismount and fight, or run?"

McCarthy didn't wait to reply. "Wheeling his horse, [he] started at full speed down the creek, losing his hat and dropping his gun," recalled Bill. "Away he went, never once looking back to see if he was being pursued."

Bill galloped after him, wanting to explain the joke. But it was no use. McCarthy reached the fort first. By the time Bill arrived, General Carr had already ordered two companies of cavalry to track down the raiders.

"I told the general that the Indians were only some Pawnee playing a joke on us," said Bill. Mischievously, he added, "I forgot to inform him that *I* had put up the trick."

The house Bill built for Lulu at Fort McPherson, c. 1870.

THE RETURN OF LULU

In the spring of 1870, Bill persuaded Lulu to live with him again. With the money he'd earned as a guide and scout, he had a small house built at Fort McPherson. Complete with a picket fence and real windows, it was, by western standards, "a wonderful thing." Lulu and three-year-old Arta soon settled into fort life. Lulu made friends with officers' wives and attended the dances and theatricals. She took in sewing, and with the extra money bought wallpaper and knickknacks. A cozy contentment filled their little home. There were fewer angry words. Fewer tears. And soon a new baby was on the way.

In November 1870, Bill arrived home from a hunting expedition to find the place overflowing with soldiers and women from the fort. An event "far greater than that of the biggest kind of Indian raid" had occurred while he was away: Lulu had given birth to their second child.

"A boy!" exclaimed Bill as he moved to his wife's bedside.

The visitors drew back so that the new parents could be alone.

Bill kissed the baby's cheek. "Daddy's boy," he murmured. "Daddy's boy."

They decided to call the baby Kit Carson Cody, in honor of the legendary scout Christopher "Kit" Carson, who had died just two years before. Bill remarked, "I want him to grow up to be a real man."

PUTTING ON A LITTLE STYLE

The following August, the richest, most influential group of sports Bill had ever guided arrived at Fort McPherson. Friends of General Sheridan, the group included James Gordon Bennett Jr., editor of the *New York Herald*; Charles L. Wilson, editor of the *Chicago Evening Journal*; and a number of other prominent businessmen, bankers, and industrialists. One member of the group later recalled that they'd come out by train to "hunt buffalo, course the antelope, shoot the wild turkey, and pursue the mighty jackrabbit in his native hills."

Wanting to make a favorable impression on the "knobby and high-toned" men, Bill decided to meet their expectations of how a "real" western guide should look: "I dressed in a new suit of buckskin, trimmed along the seams with fringes of the same material; and I put on a crimson shirt handsomely ornamented on the bosom, while on my head I wore a broad sombrero. Then mounting a snow white horse—a gallant stepper—I rode [out] . . . rifle in hand. I felt first-rate that morning, and looked well."

His appearance dazzled the group. "As his horse came toward us on an easy gallop, he realized to perfection the bold hunter and gallant sportsman of the plains," wrote one.

It was the type of costume Bill would wear ever after.

The expedition got under way, winding up Cottonwood Canyon toward the divide between the Platte and Republican Rivers. Sixteen wagons rattled along behind the hunters. One of them carried linen tablecloths, china, and crystal, all necessary items for the multicourse dinners that would be prepared by French chefs and served by waiters in evening clothes. Another wagon was solely for ice to keep the sports' wine chilled. "For years afterward," Bill recalled, "travelers recognized the [camp] sites by the quantities of empty bottles which remained behind." Five greyhounds also came along to flush out rabbits, as did one hundred cavalrymen to pull the wagons and protect the party.

With Bill leading the way, and for the next ten days, the men hunted. And hunted. And hunted. In that time, they killed six hundred buffalo, two hundred elk, and uncounted numbers of rabbits, turkeys, and prairie dogs. At the end of each day, exhausted from the slaughter, they sat down to meals that included such dishes as "buffalo tail [soup] . . . salami of prairie dog, stewed rabbit [and] . . . antelope chops." They washed it all down with perfectly chilled champagne.

The sports had a marvelous time, and they gave Bill full credit. When they urged him to visit them in New York and Chicago, Bill promised he would.

But any trip east would have to wait. Royalty was coming to the Great Plains, and General Sheridan insisted that the famous Buffalo Bill take part in the hunt.

BUFFALO BILL'S ROYAL PAIN

It was rare for royalty to come to America and rarer still for any to come west. But Grand Duke Alexis, third son of Tsar Alexander I of Russia, desired a trip to the plains. An avid hunter, he longed to shoot buffalo.

Officials in Washington gave General Sheridan the task of hosting the event. Spare no expense, they instructed, and extend every courtesy.

Sheridan immediately began putting plans in motion. Selecting a site on Red Willow Creek, fifty miles from Fort McPherson, he had soldiers pitch camp: twelve walled tents festooned with flags, as well as a larger mess tent for the planned banquets. Wagons arrived with satin comforters, bone china, and crystal glassware.

At the same time, Sheridan invited Brulé Sioux chief Spotted Tail and his people to join them at Camp Alexis, as the site was now being called. The federal government and Chief Spotted Tail had recently come to a shaky peace. Now Sheridan wanted the Brulé to show the grand duke how they hunted buffalo. He also hoped they would perform a war dance. In exchange, Sheridan promised to give ten thousand rations of flour, sugar, and coffee, as well as a thousand rations of tobacco, to every member of the band who came.

Chief Spotted Tail accepted the invitation.

During this time, Bill kicked around the fort, bored and irritable. "I had but little to do," he complained.

At last, on January 13, 1872, the grand duke's train chugged into North Platte. Bill was there to meet it. Much to his dismay, so was Lieutenant Colonel George Armstrong Custer.

The handsome thirty-two-year-old Custer—hero of the Civil War and American Indian fighter—was a celebrity with white readers back east. And Custer reveled in it. Like Bill, he cultivated his reputation as a western hero by sporting long hair and wearing a buckskin suit. But unlike Bill, Custer was vain and cruel. He flogged his men for minor offenses and shamed the offenders by ordering them to shave half their heads. "He is the most complete example of a petty tyrant I have ever seen," reported one of his junior officers. Most who knew Custer admitted he was brave. But his was a brash kind of courage, leading him to make unwise choices in hopes of catching the attention of the press.

Bill wanted as little to do with Custer as possible.

And Custer felt the same way about him. He resented Bill's rise to fame and sneeringly called him "Antelope Jim."

Now they would be together for two whole days.

Bill had put great thought into his costume for his meeting with Russian royalty. This time, because it was winter, he wore a fur-trimmed buckskin coat and a slouch hat. Once again, he sat atop a white horse.

The newspaper reporters traveling with the grand duke barely noticed. "[Custer] appeared in his well-known frontier buckskin hunting costume," wrote one. Almost as an afterthought he added, "Buffalo Bill's dress was somewhat similar to Custer's."

If that wasn't galling enough, as the group rode from the station to Camp Alexis, the grand duke asked Custer for his advice on buffalo hunting. Bill must have gritted his teeth. Alexis obviously hadn't heard about the time Custer had chased after a bison for several miles only to have the animal turn and charge him. Terrified, he'd hastily fired. He ended up shooting his horse instead of the buffalo. Luckily for him, the bison had trotted away instead of goring him. And did Custer learn his lesson? No. He'd killed two more horses in the same greenhorn way.

Now as they approached the campsite, a military band burst into a Russian hymn. Spread out behind the army tents sat 265 Brulé lodges, housing nearly 800 of Spotted Tail's people. It must have been a breathtaking sight.

Hunting began the next morning. Alexis, with both Cody and Custer at his side, trotted out of camp. Bill soon located a herd of buffalo. Custer and the grand duke charged away, leaving Bill to watch sulkily as Custer scattered the herd, then pointed out a big bull for Alexis to shoot. Revolvers blasting, the grand duke soon had his first trophy.

And Bill?

Later, when writing his autobiography, he put himself into the event, claiming that without his help Alexis would never have brought down the animal: "He fired six shots from this [pistol] at the buffalo only twenty feet away from him, but as he shot wildly not one of his bullets took effect. Seeing that the animals were bound to make their escape, I rode up to him, gave him my old reliable Lucretia . . . 'Now is your time,' said I. He fired and down went the buffalo."

This photograph of George Custer (left), Grand Duke Alexis of Russia (center), and Bill (right) is really a fake. When Custer and the grand duke had their picture taken together to commemorate the royal hunt, Cody was not invited. Instead, he posed alone. Years later, still smarting from the slight, Bill created this publicity photo by splicing his picture into that of Custer and the grand duke.

It's an entertaining story. Unfortunately, it didn't happen.

Instead, Bill spent the two-day hunt on the sidelines as Custer and Alexis, along with General Sheridan, Chief Spotted Tail, and eight other Brulé, charged after the herds he'd tracked. Altogether the men killed fifty-six buffalo. Not one of them was shot by Bill.

On the morning of January 16, Bill led the party back to the North Platte train station. A simpering Custer climbed aboard the train behind the grand duke. He'd been asked to travel to Colorado with Alexis for yet more hunting.

Bill watched the men go. Not only had the hunt been a disappointment, but it had also shown him just how minor a figure he still was compared to celebrities like Custer. To truly capitalize on his dimenovel fame, he would have to do something bold.

He would have to go to New York City.

A reenactment of the Battle of the Little Bighorn (c. 1894). Note the panoramic background and the way performers could gallop directly through the scenery.

ACT
FIVE

STARRING BUFFALO BILL
OR
"BATTLE OF THE LITTLE BIG HORN— HISTORICAL PICTURE OF CUSTER'S LAST CHARGE, MEETING AND CONSOLIDATION OF HOSTILE SIOUX ON THE BIG HORN UNDER SITTING BULL."

—Buffalo Bill's Wild West Program, 1894

A SCENE FROM THE WILD WEST

Showgoers cannot believe their eyes. A huge canvas 440 feet long and 49 feet high stretches along the back wall of the arena. On it is a realistic depiction of the endless Montana prairie as it stretches down to the edge of the Little Big-horn River. Its painted sky—vast and blue—blends into the real one above. The illusion it creates is stunning. Audience members feel transported. They feel as if they are actually looking over an expanse of western plain.

In one corner of this animated tableau two dozen performers costumed as members of the Seventh Cavalry are relaxing around a fire. In their midst sits an actor dressed as their commanding officer, Lieutenant Colonel George Armstrong Custer. The audience recognizes the Custer lookalike from the gold braid on his uniform and the blond curls flowing down around his shoulders. A few of the women in the stands sigh. How handsome Custer was!

Across the showground sits another camp. It is a group of Native per-formers acting as if they are peacefully enjoying the beauty of the prairie. Then a bugle sounds in the distance. The warriors cup their ears. Soldiers are coming! Whispering a plan, they disappear into the wings.

Only Custer and his men remain in the arena. They leap into their saddles as the bugle now sounds the charge. Raising his sword, Custer puts spurs to his stallion. He rides into the center of the arena like a cyclone, his troops following behind.

A handful of Lakota warriors now ride onto the showground. But when they see the troops, they wheel their horses and gallop away.

Have they been turned back that easily?

No, it is a trick!

As the soldiers thunder after them, a phalanx of warriors suddenly bursts from an entryway in the middle of the canvas.

The audience is astonished. Another illusion. It looks as if the Lakota are actually racing from the river's edge, thundering straight toward them, en-gulfing the cavalry as it comes. Showgoers are both thrilled and alarmed as rifles blaze and the air turns blue with gun smoke. Warriors and soldiers alike jump from their horses. They struggle with one another, grimacing and panting in hand-to-hand combat. One by one the men in blue fall. At last, only Custer remains standing. He fights bravely. But it is no use. Pressing his hand to his heart, he falls.

A sob shudders through the audience as the victors ride away.

Silence.

Then Buffalo Bill rides in, a majestic figure in the spotlight. Head bowed, he surveys the carnage. Two words flash onto the backdrop: "Too late."

Sorrowful music fills the arena. There is little cheering, less applause. The mood in the stands is suddenly mournful. "I suppose they thought they were right," says one showgoer. Others turn to their programs, where a verse from a poem by Henry Wadsworth Longfellow has been reprinted:

A melodramatic reenactment of Custer's death (c. 1894). This moment never failed to bring gasps, cries, and even boos from the white audience.

Whose was the right and the wrong?
Sing it, O funeral song,
With a voice that is full of tears,
And say that our broken faith,
Wrought all this ruin and scathe.

The words echo what Buffalo Bill himself has recently told a reporter:

The defeat of Custer was not a massacre. The Indians were being pursued by skilled fighters with orders to kill. For centuries they had been hounded . . . They had their wives and little ones to protect and they were fighting for their existence . . . In nine times out of ten when there is trouble between white men and Indians it will be found that the white man is responsible. Indians expect a man to keep his word. They can't understand how a man would lie. Most of them would cut off a leg as tell a lie.

It was a surprising statement from a man who once murdered and scalped a young Cheyenne warrior—just for publicity.

When Bill Cody, just days short of his twenty-sixth birthday, emerged from the train station that drizzling February day in 1872, he felt as if he'd stepped into another world. New York City's brick streets bustled with carriages and delivery wagons. And a line of buildings stretched as far as his eyes could see, broken only by the occasional church steeple and lines of laundry that even on this cold day twisted stiffly in the wind. "Everything [was] new and startling," he remembered.

J. G. Heckscher, one of the millionaire sports, hurried forward and hustled Bill into a carriage. The men wove their way toward fashionable Fifth Avenue. That's when Heckscher suggested they make a quick stop at his tailor's. After all, one simply could not wear buckskin to the theater. Before he knew it, Bill found himself being fitted for evening clothes—tails, top hat, even a walking stick. Standing before the mirror, Bill admitted he made "an imposing spectacle" in the getup.

It was only the beginning. Shopping. Sightseeing. Dinners and receptions in his honor. Wherever he went, well-heeled New Yorkers—especially women—crowded around him. They stared, touched his arm, and asked endless questions. Tongue-tied, Bill confessed that it was "more difficult for me to face the throng of beautiful ladies than it would have been to confront a throng of hostile Indians."

One afternoon he received a note from Ned Buntline inviting him to the theater. The author had recently turned "Buffalo Bill, the King of Border Men" into a stage play. Now he offered to reserve Bill a private box for opening night.

Bill eagerly accepted. "I was curious to see how I would look when represented by someone else," he confessed.

The night of the performance, Bill slipped into the packed theater. Fascinated, he watched as the Buffalo Bill character leaped onstage wearing a long black wig and buckskin suit. Slashing at bad guys and wrestling border ruffians, the actor kept the audience on the edge of its seat. At play's end, the audience shouted for the author.

Buntline stepped onstage. Pointing to the theater box, he introduced the "real" Buffalo Bill. "Come out . . . and make a speech," he called.

Bill declined.

But the cheering theatergoers finally convinced him to say a few words. "I found myself on stage . . . in front of an audience for the first time in my life. Everywhere I saw a sea of human faces, and thousands of eyes all staring at me." Suddenly embarrassed, Bill had no idea what to say. "I made a desperate effort and a few words escaped me, but what they were I could not for the life of me tell, nor could anyone else in the house."

No matter. Buntline knew a moneymaker when he saw one. People, he realized, would come in droves to see the hero of the West. He offered the play's role of Buffalo Bill to the real thing.

Bill turned it down. "[You] might as well make an actor out of a . . . mule," he said.

Besides, he needed to hurry home. Just that morning, he'd received a telegram from General Sheridan. Trouble was brewing, and the army needed his services.

Packing up his evening clothes, Bill boarded the first train headed west.

HONORS COME AND GO AND COME AGAIN

It began when a small party of cheated Miniconjou (one of the seven tribal bands of the Lakota) retaliated by raiding McPherson Station, killing three men and stealing a dozen horses. Ordered to track down the warriors, the Third Cavalry marched out of Fort McPherson on a clear April day in 1872. Scouting for them was Bill Cody, fresh from New York and spoiling for a fight.

At the Loup River, Bill and an advance party of six men scoured the area for signs of the warriors. Stumbling upon a trail, they followed it to where a dozen Lakota had made camp with the stolen horses. Bill and the others crept forward. They were less than fifty feet away when the warriors spotted them. Vaulting onto their horses, they made for the river.

Bill charged after them, "Lucretia Borgia" blasting.

One and then two warriors tumbled into the water as the others escaped over the riverbank. Rounding up the horses they'd ridden, Bill returned to the troops.

That evening the commanding officer wrote up the incident in his official report: "Mr. William Cody's reputation for bravery and skill as a guide is so well-established that I need not say anything else but that he acted in his usual manner."

It was hardly a heroic act. And yet on the basis of this report Bill was awarded the Medal of Honor on May 22, 1872.

Nowadays, the Medal of Honor is the country's highest military honor. Awarded sparingly, it is given for valor in combat. But in 1872 no one thought the medal was particularly special. The army awarded it all the time, and for almost any reason. One of Cody's fellow troopers received the award merely for following orders promptly and cheerfully. And, unlike today, honorees did not receive their award in a White House ceremony. They received it in the mail. So lacking in prestige was the award that even a braggart like Bill rarely mentioned it. It just didn't mean much.

Still, he *was* a Medal of Honor recipient—that is, until 1917. That year, Congress retroactively tightened the rules for receiving a Medal of Honor. One of those rules stated that only members of the military could receive the award. Since Bill had been a civilian scout, Congress stripped him of his medal. Seventy-two years later, however, it changed its mind. Deciding that Bill "nonetheless was deserving of the award," it restored his commendation in 1989.

Big Decisions

The summer of 1872 was a busy one for Bill. "I made several other scout[ing trips] . . . ," he later wrote, "with different officers of the Third Cavalry, one being with Major Alick Moore . . . with whom I was out thirty days. Another long one was with Major Curtis . . . on which trip the command ran out of rations and for fifteen days subsisted entirely on the game [I] killed."

Meanwhile, Lulu remained at home. Pregnant again and alone, she occasionally asked her friend and neighbor Orra McDonald to spend the night. Mrs. McDonald always agreed. She liked Lulu and thought five-year-old Arta and two-year-old Kit were charming. When Lulu went into labor on the morning of August 15, it was Mrs. McDonald—

not Bill—who paced the front room's floor. Hours later, the post surgeon at Fort McPherson noted: "3 p.m. Mrs. Cody . . . delivered of a daughter." A weak, delicate baby, she was christened Orra Maude after Lulu's stalwart friend.

By all accounts, Arta Cody—shown here around age ten—was a miniature of her mother, with dark hair and lustrous black eyes. She was poised beyond her years, and neighbors recalled her ability to flawlessly recite poetry at a moment's notice.

All that summer, too, Ned Buntline bombarded Bill with letters. He begged the scout to return east, go onstage, and play himself. "There is money in it," he promised. "You will [be] a big card."

Despite his earlier stage fright, the idea tempted Bill—or at least the money did. Besides, he wouldn't have to travel alone. Fellow scout John Baker "Texas Jack" Omohundro wanted to come. Tall and loose-limbed, Texas Jack was sure he, too, could become a star. "When my old 'pard' consented to try [his] luck with me in the new enterprise I felt better," admitted Bill. He decided to go.

Now all he had to do was convince Lulu.

"I don't know just how bad I'll be at actin'," he confessed to her one day in early September. "I guess maybe I'd better find out."

Lulu agreed. Tired of fort life, she wanted to take the children to her parents' home for a long visit. Besides, they needed the money. Shouldn't they be able to "send [the children] to fine schools and have everything for them that we wanted?" she asked.

So the Codys sold their house and all its furnishings. And two months later they bade farewell to Fort McPherson. Lulu and the children headed for St. Louis. Bill and Texas Jack went to Chicago.

"HURRAH, HURRAH FOR *THE SCOUTS OF THE PRAIRIE!*"

"What the deuce do you mean?" shouted the theater owner. He couldn't believe his ears. It was December 12, 1872; in just six days, Buffalo Bill and Texas Jack were expected to appear in Ned Buntline's newest stage play. The theater had been reserved. Ads had been taken out in the *Chicago Journal*. And *now* the author was telling him there was no play?

"I have not yet written [it]," Buntline explained.

The theater owner sputtered. "This will never do . . . You can't

The "Scouts of the Prairie" (c. 1873). From left to right: Ned Buntline, Buffalo Bill Cody, and Texas Jack Omohundro.

possibly write a drama, cast [actors], and rehearse it properly for Monday night . . . It [is] utterly impossible." He threatened to cancel the performance.

But Buntline remained unruffled. "Come with me, boys," he called to Bill and Jack.

The scouts, who had arrived in Chicago just hours earlier, followed him out of the theater. Down busy State Street they swept, and into the Hotel Sherman. There in a suite of rented rooms, the author put pen to paper.

"I never lay out plots in advance," Buntline once said, explaining his writing process. "First I invent a title, when I hit a good one, I consider the story about half finished . . . After I begin I push ahead as fast as I can . . . never making a correction or modification."

Four hours later, he leaped up from his desk. "Hurrah, hurrah for

The Scouts of the Prairie," he shouted. "That's the title of the play. It's finished!"

He handed Bill the script.

"I looked at my part and then at Jack; and Jack looked at his part and then at me . . . Then we [both] looked . . . at Buntline," recalled Cody.

"How long will it take to commit your part to memory, Bill?" asked Jack.

"About six months," replied Bill.

"It'll take me that [long] to learn the first line," said Jack.

Calling for the bellboy, they ordered a bottle of whiskey. Then they settled down to work.

Buntline, meanwhile, hurried out to find some other actors.

STAGE FRIGHT BEFORE THE FOOTLIGHTS

Nixon's Amphitheater filled rapidly with people. Time and again, Bill peeked through the hole in the curtain. As the crowd grew, so did his nervousness. After the curtain went up and he stepped onstage, he froze. His lines—if he'd actually memorized them—went straight out of his head. All he could do was stare at the audience, open-mouthed.

Buntline gave Cody his cue.

But the scout just stood there, fidgeting.

Desperate, Buntline prompted, "Where have you been, Bill? What has kept you so long?"

At that moment, Bill spotted W. F. Milligan in the audience. Months earlier, he'd guided Milligan on a hunt. Now the frightened actor blurted, "I've been out on a hunt with Milligan."

The audience cheered.

And Buntline, desperate to keep him talking, called out again, "Well, Bill, tell us all about that hunt."

Bill did, improvising a funny story about his hunt with the Chicagoan. Because the city's newspapers had reported the event, the audience cheered, eager for firsthand details. "I chipped in anything I thought of," remembered Bill. "In this way I took up fifteen minutes without once speaking a word of my part."

Dazed, Bill remembered little else about his premiere. Still, he realized "there was no backing out after that." Not even when critics savaged the play.

In a review published the following morning, the *Chicago Times* wondered what Buntline had been doing in the four hours he claimed to have been writing the drama. The *Inter-Ocean* regretted that a long-winded minor character who met his death in the second act hadn't died in the first. Another critic expressed the opinion that Cody was ridiculous, while Jack was "not quite so good looking, not so tall and not so ridiculous."

It didn't matter. Audiences weren't coming for the play. They were coming to see its stars. And from his first moment onstage, Bill Cody *was* a star. After a profitable week in Chicago, the troupe moved on to other cities—Cincinnati, New Haven, Boston, New York.

When *The Scouts of the Prairie* played St. Louis months later, Lulu took Arta to see it. Bill spied them sitting in the third row. Leaning over the footlights, he shouted, "Oh, Mama, I am a bad actor."

Lulu flushed with embarrassment.

But the house roared.

Ignoring his wife's discomfort, Bill blew her a kiss, then leaned forward again. "Honest, Mama, does this look as awful out there as it feels up here?"

Again, the audience roared. Then someone shouted that "Mama" was really "Mrs. Buffalo Bill." And in the next second, Lulu was being boosted onstage with Arta right behind her. Her stage fright plainly showed.

"Now you can understand how hard your poor old husband has to work to make a living," Bill boomed.

The house roared again, just like he knew it would. Regardless of what he said, Bill was growing comfortable onstage. He was discovering that audiences responded to him. He was learning to give them what they wanted.

Despite the packed theaters, when the touring season ended in June 1873, Bill's share of the profits was just six thousand dollars. Why wasn't his take more?

Lulu claimed it was due to his extravagance. She told about a time she and the children joined him in New York. They checked into a hotel only to discover that their rooms were on the noisy side of the building. Bill complained to the manager.

"The only way you could have absolute peace and quiet would be to rent the entire floor, and of course you don't want to do that," said the manager.

"Don't I . . . ," said Bill. "How much is it?"

The manager replied that it would cost two hundred dollars (approximately thirty-five hundred dollars in today's money). It was a steep price to pay for peace and quiet.

But Bill, ignoring his wife's protests, cried, "Paid! Now let's see how quick you can make things comfortable for us. I've got a wife and babies and we're all tired."

It was the start of a pattern—periods of prosperity followed by reckless extravagance—that he would follow the rest of his life.

Bill, however, blamed Ned Buntline for his lack of fortune. Convinced the writer had cheated him, he decided to form his own acting troupe.

But first, he was going hunting. "Texas Jack and myself longed for . . . the western prairies once more," he said. The scouts-turned-actors headed for Fort McPherson.

Lulu and the children remained back east. While traveling in New York, Lulu had taken a liking to Rochester. Now she and the children settled into a comfortable house on Exchange Street. She waited there, as always, for her husband's return.

SEASONS ONSTAGE

For the next five years Bill would divide his life between East and West. In the fall he put on a play, or what was then called a "combination." Hiring a group of actors, he toured the country performing melodramatic stories with titles such as *The Prairie Waif*; *Buffalo Bill at Bay; or, The Pearl of the Prairies*; and *From Noose to Neck*. Advertisements for these performances promised "a thrilling picture of western border life."

While he was on tour, Bill's days were a string of stuffy hotel rooms and dusty railroad seats. When he wasn't onstage, he was attending to business—arranging for theaters, paying actors, dealing with publicity, and counting box office receipts. And the receipts were good. In those first years, the Buffalo Bill Combination earned as much in a week as Bill himself did in a whole year of scouting.

Then came summer. Leaving the theater as well as his family behind, Bill headed west. Back in the saddle, he guided hunting parties and did a bit of scouting. He considered these months his vacation. But they had even more important purposes: they reinforced his reputation as a real frontiersman and provided new material for the following theatrical season. When Bill returned to the stage in the fall, audiences flocked to see him reenact his summer exploits. They took him for the real thing. And so he was.

"A BEAUTIFUL ANGEL IN THAT BETTER WORLD"

On April 20, 1876, just as Bill was stepping onto a Springfield, Massachusetts, stage, someone handed him a telegram. Five-year-old Kit

Carson Cody was seriously ill with scarlet fever. Bill needed to hurry to Rochester.

Somehow, he bumbled through the first act. Then leaving his manager, John Burke, to play out his part, he sprinted to catch the evening train.

It was a long, anxious ride. As the train chugged through the darkness, Bill must have replayed memories of his son over and over in his mind. Did he recall the time the boy had attended one of his performances? Knowing how important a large audience was to his father, Kit had anxiously watched the theater fill up. When Bill appeared onstage, the boy had cupped his mouth and called out, "Good house, Papa." The delighted audience had applauded, and Bill had swelled with pride. He had such high hopes for the handsome little rascal. He prayed now that the boy would survive.

At last, early the next morning, he arrived in Rochester. Racing to the house, he found Kit alive but unable to speak. Still, "he seemed to recognize me," said Bill, "and putting his little arms around my neck he tried to kiss me." All day, the doctor came and went. Lulu sponged the boy's feverish brow. Bill clutched his tiny hand. "But it was of no avail," he recalled. "That evening at six o'clock my beloved little Kit died in my arms."

Bill struggled to understand the tragedy. Writing to his sister Julia at three o'clock in the morning—just hours

The only known photograph of Kit Carson Cody, taken in 1876, the year he died. Holding the little rifle made especially for him, Kit wears his hair shoulder length, just like his famous father.

after Kit's death—he told her, "God wanted him where he could live in a better world . . . And now his place is vacant and can never be filled, for he has gone to be a beautiful angel in that better world, where he will wait for us."

Days after Kit's death, Bill returned to the theater. But his heart wasn't in it. So when he received a letter from Brevet Lieutenant Colonel Anson Mills urging him to return to the plains, he jumped at the chance. Abandoning Lulu to deal with her grief by herself, he closed his touring season early. He was off, he told audiences, "to fight real Indians." Rejoining the Fifth Cavalry at Cheyenne, Wyoming, in June, he arrived just as events reached a boiling point.

CUSTER'S LAST STAND

Gold! According to all reports, the Black Hills, located in the Dakota Territory, practically glittered with the precious stuff. But the land belonged to the Lakota. Seven years earlier, the federal government had signed a treaty with this group granting "absolute and undisturbed use and occupation of the Black Hills."

To the Lakota, these hills have always been sacred. They were also what Hunkpapa warrior and holy man Sitting Bull called a "food pack." The valleys overflowed with game, and the slopes were covered with trees for winter fuel. Sitting Bull believed the Black Hills were the last place where his people could preserve the old ways. If they lost them to the settlers, they would no longer be able to live as true Lakota.

But with reports of gold, settlers swarmed into the Black Hills. Ignoring the treaty, they threw up mining camps and towns. The government did little to stop them.

Desperate, the Lakota and Cheyenne people had no choice but to join forces. Many who lived on reservations rode off to join those who still did not. Together they vowed to drive out the intruders.

The federal government, in turn, ordered *all* the tribes onto reservations—or else.

The tribes refused to obey. They spread out across the region.

A furious General Sheridan ordered Custer and the Seventh Cavalry to crush them.

On June 15, 1876, Custer's forces—six hundred men strong—located a three-mile-long encampment in the valley of a winding stream called the Little Bighorn. Custer had been ordered to wait for reinforcements before attacking. But impulsive and arrogant, he wanted to strike on his own. Without knowing what the terrain looked like, or how many warriors there were, he charged.

It was a quiet day in the encampment. The dances the night before hadn't ended until sunrise, and many people had slept late. As the afternoon grew hot, a group of adults and children took to the river. They splashed and played while a cluster of men smoked and relaxed in the big lodge. Good White Buffalo Woman poked up her cooking fire. "The Sioux that [day] had no thought of fighting," she later said. "We expected no attack."

Then two boys ran into camp. "Soldiers are coming!" they cried. Calm gave way to chaos. Shouting and crying, swimmers rushed from the water. Women gathered their children and dashed for cover. Then came the sound of bullets "like hail on tepees and tree tops," recalled Hunkpapa warrior Little Soldier. The warriors—more than two thousand Hunkpapa, Oglala, Miniconjou, Sans Arc, Sihasapa, and Northern Cheyenne in all—raced for their horses and weapons. Led by Chiefs Crazy Horse, Gall, and Lame White Man, the warriors descended on Custer's troops. As one warrior remembered, "The battle lasted no longer than a hungry man needs to eat his dinner." When it was over, 268 soldiers lay dead, including Custer.

The victorious warriors rejoiced. They had killed the man who had invaded their home and tried to destroy their families.

It was Custer's last stand.

THE FIRST SCALP FOR CUSTER

Cody and the Fifth Cavalry were scouting the country around Wyoming's Sage Creek, 150 miles northwest of the Little Bighorn, when news of Custer's death arrived. Bill quickly realized that the Plains Wars now had a "genuine battlefield martyr," that Custer would become a symbol of the white man's struggle to conquer the frontier. Bill also realized that all eyes would be on the West. The white citizens

BUFFALO BILL—COL. WILLIAM F. CODY

Bill poses for a publicity shot (c. 1877) in the black velvet jacket he wore when he killed Yellow Hair.

would want revenge. And this provided an opportunity. Here was a chance to tie his name to Custer's. But how?

He soon hit on an idea.

The next morning, Bill dressed in one of his most flamboyant stage costumes: a black velvet jacket, a red silk shirt trimmed with silver buttons and lace, and a pair of trousers—also velvet—that flared at the knee.

The soldiers must have chuckled at his strange outfit, but Bill didn't care. He knew there was bound to be a fight soon. And he wanted to be able to tell his theater audiences that *this* was the actual suit he'd worn in battle.

The Fifth Cavalry headed out. As Bill tells it, the command had gotten word that eight hundred Cheyenne had broken from the Red Cloud Agency at Fort Robinson, Nebraska, and were headed north to join Crazy Horse. The Fifth's mission was to stop them.

On July 17, at Warbonnet Creek (on the border between Wyoming and Nebraska), Bill spotted a small band of Cheyenne while out scouting with Colonel Wesley Merritt and a half dozen men. Scout and soldiers galloped over the bluff to cut them off. Said Bill, "A running fight lasted several minutes, during which we drove the enemy some distance and killed three of their number."

The remaining Cheyenne fled. But at the top of a ridge, they met up with the rest of their band—"a large party," said Bill, "that had just come into sight." Inexplicably, the eight hundred Cheyenne stopped in their tracks when they saw the half dozen soldiers and their weirdly dressed scout. Then the fleeing Cheyenne suddenly turned back.

"I know you, Pa-he-haska," a subchief named Yellow Hair supposedly called out, using the name the Cheyenne had given Bill. "If you want to fight, come ahead and fight me." He rode his horse back and forth in front of his men, goading Bill.

What else could the scout do?

"I . . . accepted his challenge," he said.

According to Bill, the men galloped toward each other at top speed like jousting knights of medieval times. When they were within feet of one another, they raised their rifles and fired.

Yellow Hair's horse fell to the ground, killed by Bill's bullet.

At the same time, Cody's horse went down after stepping in a hole. Both men rolled to their feet.

"We fired at each other simultaneously," claimed Bill. "His bullet missed me, while mine struck him in the breast. He reeled and fell."

Thinking of his white audiences, Cody leaped onto Yellow Hair's chest. Bill "jerk[ed] the Indian's warbonnet off, [and] scientifically scalped him in about five minutes." This was the first and only time in his life that he had scalped anyone.

Just then, the rest of Merritt's company came charging over the hill. As the soldiers galloped toward him, Bill theatrically swung Yellow Hair's topknot in the air. "The first scalp for Custer!" he shouted.

The troops cheered. Then they tore after the Cheyenne. "It was no use for any eight hundred . . . Indians to try and check a charge of the gallant old Fifth Cavalry, and they soon . . . began a running retreat towards Red Cloud Agency," Bill concluded smugly.

The next day, he wrote to Lulu bragging about his exploits, promising to send Yellow Hair's warbonnet, shield, bridle, whip, and scalp. He wanted his Rochester friend Moses Kerngood to display them in his cigar store window.

The package arrived before the letter. Thinking her husband had sent a gift, Lulu eagerly pried off the lid. A terrible smell wafted out. "I reeled slightly, reached for the contents, and then fainted," she recalled.

When she recovered, she took a closer look. Nestled beside the warbonnet made of eagle feathers and buffalo skin lay a two-foot-long braid of straight black hair attached to a three-inch-wide square of scalp.

Days later, the items appeared in Kerngood's store window. They remained there—ogled by Rochester's citizens—until Bill returned in September. All that following season, his combination performed a reenactment of that fight on Warbonnet Creek to sold-out theaters across the East. Bill always wore his velvet suit. He always held up Yellow Hair's topknot. And he always hollered, "The first scalp for Custer!"

Evidence of Bill's terrible deed on display in a Rochester, New York, storefront (c. 1877).

How much of Bill's story is true? His version of Yellow Hair's death has raised questions ever since he began reenacting it in 1876. No one doubts he killed the Cheyenne subchief. Yet the circumstances surrounding the event remain murky.

In his autobiography Bill claimed that the Fifth Cavalry had been ordered north to chase eight hundred renegade Cheyenne. But historical records show that only two hundred Native people were at the Red Cloud Agency in July 1876, and only a small number of them rode off. Curiously, not a single army report mentions ever seeing more than thirty warriors on the day of the skirmish. And Colonel Merritt admitted to spotting just seven—a far cry from the eight hundred Bill claimed rode over the ridge. Why inflate the numbers? There can be just one reason. Bill hoped to turn a minor skirmish into a major event—and a fair fight.

As for the fight itself, most historians find Bill's version ludicrous. They point out that the idea of a duel similar to a medieval jousting tournament would have been completely unknown in Cheyenne warfare. American Indians simply did not fight like that.

Additionally, Cody implied that Yellow Hair knew him. But Bill had never faced the Northern Cheyenne in battle before. Neither the subchief nor his band could have recognized Bill. Equally farfetched is the notion that his reputation was so notorious that the Cheyenne had given him the name Pa-he-haska (supposedly meaning "long hair"). It's far more likely that Cody made it all up to enhance his reputation with eastern audiences.

Finally, there is the matter of Yellow Hair calling out to him. Bill claimed he understood what the subchief was saying. But although Cody did understand a bit of the Lakota language, he did not speak a word of Cheyenne. It would have been impossible for the men to communicate.

So what really happened between Cody and Yellow Hair?

The most reliable account comes from army signalman Chris Madsen, who watched it all through a telescope atop a neighboring hill. "From the manner in which both parties acted," Madsen wrote, "it was certain that both were surprised . . . There was no conversation, no preliminary agreement . . . They met by accident and fired the moment they faced each other. Cody's bullet went through the Indian's leg and killed his pinto pony. The Indian's bullet went wild . . . Cody jumped clear of his mount. Kneeling, he took deliberate aim and fired the second shot . . . [It] ended the battle. Cody went over to the fallen Indian and neatly removed his scalp."

A reporter from a small Kansas newspaper, the *Ellis County Star*, was also there that day. He filed a story that was much the same as Madsen's, only more flowery: "The Indian . . . turned savagely on Buffalo Bill . . . Cody cooly knelt, and taking a deliberate aim, sent the bullet through the chief's leg and his horse's head. Down went the two, and before his friends could reach him, a second shot laid the [Indian] low."

No large group of Cheyenne. No goading from Yellow Hair in any language. No joust-style duel. Just an accidental meeting followed by a grisly act that made Buffalo Bill famous.

"AIN'T THAT A NICE WAY
FOR A WIFE TO ACT?"

North Platte, Nebraska, was still a frontier town when Lulu and little Orra stepped off the train in February 1878. (Arta was in boarding school back east.) Simple houses lined dirt streets, and wooden planks thrown across the muddiest intersections served as sidewalks. There were no trees anywhere in town, and in the summer no flowers or lawns. Still, North Platte had a two-story courthouse, a brand-new schoolhouse, and plenty of shops, including bakeries, meat markets, jewelry and hardware stores, and the Star Clothing House, where men could buy long underwear.

Clutching Orra's hand and raising her own skirts above the mud, Lulu picked her way along Front Street. Why in heaven's name had she

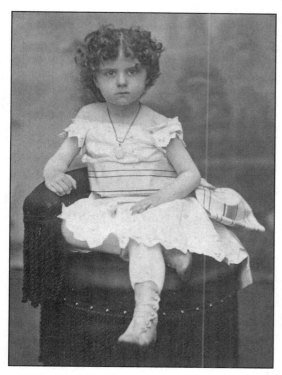

Four-year-old Orra Cody in 1876. Despite her delicate condition, Orra was a happy child who loved birthday parties, carriage rides, and the annual summer trip to Rochester, New York, where she'd get a chance to spend time with her father.

returned to the West? Because Bill had purchased land here—160 acres of prime grazing pasture. He wanted to make North Platte his hometown. But first he needed a proper house. Lulu was there to make sure he got one.

"We had money, plenty of it," she recalled. And so she didn't scrimp. "The lumber [for the house] had been hauled clear across the country [and] the furnishing came all the way from Chicago and New York." The result was "a house that was little less than a mansion," bragged Lulu. Called Welcome Wigwam by the locals, it boasted tall windows, an airy front porch, and a picket fence to keep wandering livestock out of the yard.

Bill arrived in May. He admired the house. But it was Lulu's delight in the place that pleased him most. He decided to stay a few weeks. "My long and continued absence from home made me a . . . stranger under my own roof," he admitted. For the first time in years, the Codys whiled away the days together, taking carriage rides, picking grapes, and hunting for arrowheads.

But things once again grew sour between the couple. Lulu resented Bill's theater career. Without a husband for months at a stretch, she alone took care of home and children. Particularly stressful was Orra's health. Never robust, the little girl coughed often and tired easily. Now in North Platte, Lulu felt even more burdened. "I attended to the thousand and one details of life that must be looked over, while he was away, *always* away," she complained.

Bill, meanwhile, claimed Lulu was a snob, disapproving of the stage and its customs. Jealous of his actresses, she was forever peppering him with accusatory questions. During his years onstage, she kept him "very much riled up," he said. "In fact, it was a kind of cat and dog's life all along the whole trail."

One of the worst blows to the marriage happened in 1882. That's when Bill learned that Lulu had put all his North Platte property, including the house, in her name. She claimed that this was due to Bill's impulsive spending, that she was trying to protect their financial future.

But Bill saw it differently. "Ain't that a nice way for a wife to act?" he wrote to his sister Julia. "I don't care a snap for the money, but the way she has treated me. My beautiful house. I have none to go to . . . I will have to build another."

So he did. Buying up land along the railroad tracks near North Platte, he established a ranch. Besides hundreds of horses and cattle, there were orchards and alfalfa fields, and later a graceful three-story mansion with gingerbread trim and wide porches. The ranch's centerpiece, however, would be its barn. A big, sprawling structure, it sat facing the tracks. Painted across its roof in letters that could easily be seen by train passengers was the name he chose for the ranch: Scout's Rest. This way, folks would be sure to recognize the place as belonging to the famous Buffalo Bill.

Lulu, however, refused to live at the ranch. She stayed in her house in North Platte. And even though another daughter, Irma, was born in February 1883, Bill and Lulu grew angrier and more suspicious of each other. From that time on, they rarely lived together.

COWBOY FUN

By 1882, Bill owned forty-five hundred head of cattle and four thousand acres of land. But he never did much ranching. Away too often, he hired others to manage Scout's Rest. Still, he liked to return for the annual spring roundup. That's when the local ranchmen rounded up all the cattle that had been scattered across vast tracts of land during the winter. Driving them toward a common center, each owner separated out his stock and herded his cattle to his own ranch.

The roundup bosses tolerated Bill. They let him chase and rope a few

These two modern-day photographs of the barn and house at Scout's Rest Ranch show the place looking much as it did when Bill lived there.

steers. But they kept him far away from the calves and their mothers, because all his whooping and whirling and theatrical shenanigans scared the babies. Inevitably, recalled one roundup boss, "I had to call Cody out" to get him away from the cattle. Bill didn't mind. "There is nothing but hard work on these round ups . . . ," he said. "I could not possibly find out where the fun came in."

The cowboys, however, made their own fun. Bronco riding, roping, and horse racing were all part of the roundup. And to pass the long hours in the saddle, they often played a game called pickup. Galloping at full speed, they plucked coins or pieces of paper off the ground. Their horsemanship and cowboy skills impressed Bill. He watched and remembered.

A "CRACKIN' GOOD" IDEA

In New York City in spring 1882, above the clang and clatter of Brooklyn's busy streets, Bill Cody heard someone calling his name. Turning, he saw a skinny man with a meticulously trimmed beard waving a black plug hat. Bill grinned. It was an old pal of his, the successful actor-manager-promoter Nate Salsbury.

The men shook hands. Then Salsbury asked if Bill had time for lunch. There was a matter he wanted to discuss. Since Bill didn't need to be onstage for hours, he agreed.

The men set off for a nearby restaurant. Once seated, Salsbury came right to the point. He had an idea, he said. A big idea for an outdoor show with Cody as its central figure. The show, he went on, "would encompass the whole subject of horsemanship."

Bill agreed it was a good idea. But, he suggested, what about adding some bronco busting or roping or maybe some fancy shooting?

In a flurry of creative excitement, the two made elaborate plans. "We mapped out a show . . . that had never before been [tried] in the history of show business," recalled Salsbury. Then reality set in. It would take a lot of money to do the thing right. Bill figured he could scrape together half the amount. But not Salsbury. "I did not feel rich enough to undertake my share," he admitted. The men agreed to hold off.

But the idea never quit Bill's mind. He mulled the possibilities. He rolled plans around in his head. The show, he decided, "would not smack of a circus," but would be "on a high-toned basis." Performances would be thrilling, but not too violent. This, he reasoned, would draw "the better class of people." Additionally, nothing in his show would be fake. All the "representations of life in the far west" would be performed "by the originals themselves." And their acts would astonish. Speaking to a newspaper reporter around this time, he declared, "There will be an Indian fight on horseback, and a buffalo hunt and other exciting features never yet seen in public."

The more he thought about it, the more excited he grew. "All those people back east want to find out just what the west looks like," he explained to a skeptical Lulu. "You can't [show] them something that big on a theater's stage. So why not take the west to them?"

It was a "crackin' good" idea.

Now all he needed was a partner with cash.

A SHARPSHOOTIN' DENTIST

Early in 1883, almost a year after his lunch with Nate Salsbury, Bill was having his boots polished in a Cincinnati hotel when he happened to look up. There, stomping across the lobby, was none other than William Frank "Doc" Carver.

Bill had met Carver in 1874 when he'd guided him on a hunting trip. Carver had been a dentist from Illinois back then. But the frontier life had gotten under his skin. Moving to Nebraska, he took to wearing buckskin suits and a broad-brimmed hat. He gave up dentistry and instead spent his days practicing marksmanship. Soon he was a crack shot. By 1878 he was performing for audiences in the eastern United States as well as in Europe. He won shooting matches, awards, and acclaim. He also made a fortune. And now, as luck would have it, here he was in the same hotel as Bill.

Bill called out to his brother hunter, and the two headed off to a nearby saloon. After a few hands of poker and several shots of whiskey, Bill outlined his plans for an outdoor exhibition. Did Carver want in?

He sure did. "I invested $27,000 in the enterprise," recalled Carver.

Now Bill sent a telegram to Nate Salsbury, who was in Europe.

"He asked if I wanted to go into the show . . . *if Dr. Carver did not object,*" recalled Salsbury. It was a condition Salsbury could not abide. He had no use for Carver, considering him a "fakir in show business." Salsbury turned them down.

THE WILD WEST IS BORN

In April 1883, Bill said goodbye to the stage and hurried home. He had a big show to put together. And he had to do it fast. Opening night for his new entertainment was less than a month away!

He wasn't starting completely from scratch. Over the past few months he'd collected livestock and equipment for the show. He'd already acquired a stagecoach, covered wagons, bucking horses, a herd of buffalo, and some elk and mountain sheep. He'd also signed on thirty-six Pawnee men as well as a dozen Mexican vaqueros skilled in lasso throwing. Still, there was plenty more to do. And Doc Carver was no help. Claiming to be busy back east, he refused to travel to North Platte. Luckily, Bill had plenty of friends eager to pitch in.

His neighbor William Sweeney, who'd played the coronet in the military band at Fort McPherson, offered to put together a cowboy band for the show. Gathering the best musicians in three counties, he costumed them in sombreros and neckerchiefs, then rehearsed them night and day.

Buck Taylor, a cowboy on Bill's ranch, also agreed to take part. Buck could throw a steer by the horns, pick up a coin from the ground while riding a horse at full speed, and ride the wildest of bucking broncos. Bill dubbed him "King of the Cowboys."

Con Groner, billed as the "Cowboy Sheriff of the Platte," signed on, too. The county sheriff for more than a decade, Groner was credited with catching "over fifty murderers [and even] more horse thieves, cattle rustlers, burglars and outlaws."

And then there was thirteen-year-old Johnny Baker. Johnny couldn't rope a steer or drive a stagecoach, but he adored Bill Cody. Whenever the showman was in town, the boy hung around wide-eyed, listening to Bill's stories of the plains.

Now Johnny dogged his hero and begged to go along in the show.

"What would you do in a wild west show, Johnny?" Bill asked.

"Well, I could black your boots—and—and—make myself awful handy," he replied.

Bill laughed. He had a real affection for Johnny, who was the same age that his son, Kit, would have been. He'd taught the boy to shoot and had even offered to adopt him. But Johnny's parents had said no. They did, however, agree to let him go with the show. He went as Bill's foster son.

At last, after weeks of organizing and assembling, the show was loaded onto the train in May 1883. It filled six boxcars and seven passenger cars. Bill turned to the crowd of citizens who'd gathered at the station to see him off. "I will not only exhibit my show in every state capital in the United States, but also in Washington D.C. and some capitals in Europe," he vowed.

His words caused a ripple of laughter, and someone piped up, "That's a hell of a lot of wind, even for Bill Cody."

Then with a shrill blast of its whistle and a cloud of steam, the train lurched out of the station. "The Wild West, Honorable W. F. Cody and Dr. W. F. Carver's Rocky Mountain and Prairie Exhibition"—or simply "The Wild West," as most people called it—was on its way.

Formal portrait of Annie Oakley (1899) posing with her L. C. Smith shotgun and wearing some of the sharpshooting medals she won over the years.

ACT

SIX

ROOTIN', TOOTIN', ROPIN', AND SHOOTIN'
OR
"MISS ANNIE OAKLEY, CELEBRATED SHOT, WHO WILL ILLUSTRATE HER DEXTERITY IN THE USE OF FIREARMS."

—Buffalo Bill's Wild West Program, 1894

A SCENE FROM THE WILD WEST

A small, slender woman dressed in a flower-embroidered skirt, pearl button leggings, and a wide-brimmed sombrero skips into the arena. She waves, curtsies, and blows kisses to the audience.

Many in the stands waft kisses back. How can they resist? Standing before them is America's sweetheart, the celebrated female sharpshooter Annie Oakley, or "Little Sure Shot."

Annie moves toward a table covered with rifles and shotguns. At her signal, her husband and assistant, Frank Butler, tosses a hollow glass ball the size of an orange high into the air. Annie whirls into action. Jumping over the table, she scoops up a shotgun, aims, and shoots.

Bang!

The ball shatters.

Other balls are tossed. Lots of balls. The air shimmers with them. Annie grabs up a pistol in her left hand and one in her right. She blasts every target, tossing the guns onto the table as she uses up their ammunition. Glass shards shower down.

Next Frank launches a flock of clay birds into the sky. The saucer-shaped discs soar above the showground, singly at first, then in pairs, triplets, and finally four at a time.

Holding a rifle upside down over her head, Annie wipes out every one.

Bang! Bang! Bang!

Then she does it again, this time lying on her back across a chair.

Bang! Bang! Bang!

Her shots come faster and faster.

A few of the more timid spectators cry out and cover their ears. Most, however, shout, "Bravo! Bravo!"

Annie curtsies prettily, then searches among the guns for the prop she uses in her most famous stunt—the mirror trick. With a rifle held backward over her shoulder, she sights in the mirror. Frank holds out a dime between his thumb and forefinger.

Bang!

She drills clean through it.

He lights a cigarette and places it between his lips.

Bang!

She shoots off its ember.

He holds out a small card, two inches by five inches.

Annie's gun barks.

And Frank tosses the card into the stands.

A lucky showgoer snatches it. On one end of the card is a photograph of Annie; on the other is a heart-shaped bull's-eye—with a bullet hole through its center.

The audience stands and cheers.

Annie tosses her last smoking gun onto the table, blows another kiss to the audience, and races across the arena. But just before she disappears behind the white canvas curtain, she smiles and gives an endearing little kick.

Charmed and astonished, showgoers stay on their feet even after she's gone. She is one of the show's biggest stars. And Buffalo Bill knows it. Without Little Sure Shot, the Wild West might have gone the way of the buffalo—vanished forever.

A RUNAWAY STAGECOACH AND A RUNAWAY SHOW

When Pap Clothier, mayor of Colville, Nebraska, received Bill Cody's invitation to ride in the Deadwood stagecoach during the Wild West's first-ever dress rehearsal, he was thrilled. As Bill had explained it, the attack on the stagecoach was intended to be a centerpiece of the show. Anyone riding in it for the very first performance

Bill standing in front of the famous Deadwood stagecoach (c. 1887) while driver John Y. Nelson perches on top and unidentified passengers sit inside.

was bound to go down in history. Bill also figured it would make for good publicity.

What Bill didn't explain was that everything connected with his new show was authentic. The stagecoach really had once run the route between Deadwood, South Dakota, and Cheyenne, Wyoming. And the four mules pulling it really were fresh from the West, "hard and wild and barely broken to the harness."

Bill wanted his performers to act authentic, too. "Attack and rescue like you would on the frontier," he instructed them. The only things not allowed, he added, were "killing and scalping."

On the afternoon of May 14, 1883, a puffed-up Mayor Clothier arrived at the showground. Grinning, he bowed to the crowd of spectators who'd gathered to watch the rehearsal. The Deadwood stagecoach careened toward him across the arena. By snapping a whip above the wild-eyed mules' heads and stamping his foot hard on the brake, the driver just barely managed to bring the rig to a stop.

Mayor Clothier hopped in.

And the coach hurtled off, making two rapid passes around the arena.

From its window, the mayor waved to the crowd.

The crowd cheered and waved back.

And the mules grew even more wild-eyed. They picked up their pace.

On the third pass, a group of Pawnee performers, painted and feathered, burst from their hiding place. Both the mayor and the crowd had expected the attack. But no one had told the nervous mules. As the Pawnee pounded after the rig, shouting and firing blanks, the mules bolted.

Bill had wanted real. And now he had it—a real runaway stagecoach!

Knowing he couldn't stop the fear-crazed mules, the stagecoach driver concentrated on simply keeping the lurching rig from tipping over.

Meanwhile, the Pawnee—delighted with their ambush—kept chasing the coach.

Four times around.

What to do?

Bill and his rescue party dashed into the arena. Forgetting about the rehearsal, they tried to head off both mules and Pawnee. This merely added to the chaos.

As the stagecoach careened past the crowd for the fifth time, Mayor Clothier stuck his head out the window. "Stop!" he shouted. "Hell: stop—let [me] out."

The driver couldn't.

Six times around—seven. At last the mules wore themselves out. The stagecoach rolled to a stop.

The shaky mayor burst from the rig. Fists clenched, he made for Bill. But one of the performers got there first. Pulling Bill aside, he said, "If you want to make this . . . show go, you do not need me or [those] Indians." Hire some old men, he went on, and "fix them up with all the paint and feathers on the market. Use some old hack horses and a hack driver. To make it go, you want a show of illusion, not realism."

Bill agreed it was a bumpy start. But he wasn't about to fake his show. With time, he figured, things would iron themselves out.

They didn't. At the show's opening performance in Omaha, Nebraska, three days later, the sharpshooter Doc Carver—still reeling from too much whiskey the night before—missed most of the targets. The audience booed. What kind of marksman missed every shot? They shouted, "Cody! Cody! Cody!"

Bill hadn't intended to be the show's sharpshooter. But what could he do? Obliging the spectators, he borrowed an exhibition rifle and shot rings around Carver. Jealous, the former dentist flew into a rage. Smashing his rifle in half, he stomped off the fairgrounds.

From then on, the program listed Cody as doing "novel and extraordinary shooting on foot and on horseback."

The "all-round shot" Buffalo Bill Cody blasts glass balls from the sky with the help of an American Indian who rides beside him, tossing the targets into the air (1907).

The show moved eastward. Springfield, Missouri. Council Bluffs, Iowa. Youngstown, Ohio. Pittsburgh, Pennsylvania.

"From all outward appearances," one of the show's press agents, Dexter Fellows, later wrote, "the show was a 'wow.'" Newspapers proclaimed it "a sure-fire, good time crowd pleaser."

The performers—all hardboiled frontiersmen—were having a sure-fire good time, too. "When they weren't performing, they were breaking all records for whooping it up," recalled Fellows. Of the show's sixteen train cars, he added, "one whole car was devoted to a stock of liquor." And whenever the show pulled into a town, the performers made a beeline for the closest saloon.

Bill went along, too. "He would be in the thickest of the celebration," recalled Lulu, "whooping it up as long as anyone else—and sometimes a bit longer."

While Bill's drinking didn't hurt his performances, it did affect his business practices. For almost a decade he'd managed a traveling troupe of actors, arranging for theaters, advertising, and transportation. He'd done it well and made a profit. But now he let details slide. He didn't bother to count ticket sales. He didn't push his troupers to rehearse. "It was an eternal gamble whether the show would exist from one day to the next," admitted Lulu, "not because of a lack of money, but simply [because he] stayed awake twenty hours out of twenty-four . . . celebrating."

Perhaps he drank so much because his family life was unraveling. Convinced Lulu was out to ruin him financially, Bill decided that summer to divorce her. "I have put up with that woman as long as I am going to," he told his sister Julia in September 1883.

But before he could take legal steps, he received a telegram from home. Eleven-year-old Orra, always so frail and sickly, had died on October 24.

Heartbroken, Bill hurried to North Platte. Then he and Lulu traveled with Orra's tiny body to Rochester, New York. There, in a grave strewn with evergreen branches and flowers, they buried her beside her brother, Kit. "If it was not for the hope of heaven and again meeting there, my [grief] would be more than I could bear," mourned Lulu.

Bill couldn't bring himself to tear apart the family any further. Pushing aside all thoughts of divorce, the grieving showman met up with the Wild West in Chicago. He was tired. Tired of his business partner's rages and jealousy. Tired of struggling to manage the show alone. Tired of worrying about money. It was time to move on, without Doc Carver.

Coincidentally, Nate Salsbury was also playing in Chicago. "Cody came to see me," Nate later recalled. "[He] said that if I did not take hold of the show he was going to quit the whole thing. He said . . . he would never go through another summer with Carver for a hundred thousand dollars."

Would Salsbury consider a partnership? asked Bill.

On one condition, replied Nate. Bill had to stop drinking during the show's tour season.

Bill agreed: "I solemnly promise you that after this you will never see me under the influence of liquor . . . [T]his drinking surely ends today, and your pard will be himself [and] on the deck all the time." It was a promise the showman kept.

All that remained now was to tell Carver.

The sharpshooter did not take the news well. He stormed and cursed and vowed to make *his* Wild West the most successful outdoor event ever. And he would start by taking *his* half of the show on a winter tour. But how to divide the property?

They did it the frontier way, by flipping a silver dollar. Recalled one eyewitness, the men tossed the coin and "chose in turn horse and horse, steer and steer, wagon and wagon." In one lucky toss, Bill won the Deadwood stagecoach. The rig would become one of the most continuing features of the show.

SUNK, SOAKED, AND DISGUSTED

By the spring of 1884, the new and reorganized Wild West headed out on tour. Buck Taylor, King of the Cowboys, was back. So were Con Groner and Johnny Baker, who, now fourteen, was learning to shoot in hopes of becoming a performer. "Nearly one hundred Indians, from several tribes were engaged," recalled Bill, as well as "many noted plainsmen . . . We also captured a herd of elk, a dozen buffaloes and some bears."

Buffalo Bill's Wild West opened in St. Louis in April 1884 and two weeks later packed in a crowd for a single performance at Chicago's Driving Park. By June it had reached the Polo Grounds in New York City. All along its way, critics praised the show, especially Bill's performance. In Connecticut the *Hartford Courant* gushed, "Mounted on his blooded [i.e., purebred] horse . . . Cody is an extraordinary figure, and sits on a horse as if he was born in the saddle. His feats of shooting are perfectly wonderful."

Despite the crowds and rave reviews, the Wild West made little money. That's because moving the show from place to place by train to play one-night stands was expensive. By fall the partners were almost broke. So Nate Salsbury took his former theater troupe back on the road in order to earn some badly needed cash. Meanwhile, Bill put the Wild West on a steamboat and headed down the Mississippi, playing at riverside towns along the way to cover the travel expenses. Once the show reached New Orleans, he planned on setting up a more permanent show arena, one in which they could play until the following spring.

All went according to plan until the steamboat carrying the show neared Rodney Landing, Mississippi.

Crash!

The steamboat collided with another paddle wheeler. In less than an hour, Cody's boat sank to the bottom of the river. With it went wagons, camp equipment, scenery, costumes, and props. Thrashing about in the churning water, cast and crew managed to save the show's horses and all but one elk. They also dragged the Deadwood stagecoach ashore.

Dripping and dispirited, Bill hitched a ride into the nearest town. At the telegraph office, he wired Nate: "OUTFIT AT BOTTOM OF RIVER. WHAT DO YOU ADVISE?"

Nate wired back: "GO TO NEW ORLEANS, REORGANIZE, AND OPEN ON YOUR DATE. HAVE SENT FUNDS."

Bill collected the wired money and, working around the clock, bought new livestock, replaced equipment, rented an outdoor showground, and began advertising. "We opened on [time]," he said proudly.

But things did not dry out. Every morning, the Wild West awoke to bright Louisiana sunshine. But by ten thirty, just an hour before showtime, storm clouds scuttled across the sky. Thunder rumbled and lightning flashed. Then the rain pounded down, turning the showground into a muddy mess. At four o'clock, just at show's end, the clouds parted and the sun came out once more.

It went on like this for forty-four days.

By the end of that soggy winter, the Wild West was sixty thousand dollars in the hole and Bill was beside himself. "The camel's back is broken," he wailed to Nate. "It's plain to me. I can read it clearly. *Fate* . . . is against me . . . I am thoroughly discouraged [and] . . . disgusted with myself and the world."

It looked as though the Wild West was all washed up.

Then on a wet, gray afternoon in early April 1885, a petite

twenty-five-year-old dropped by the showground. Her name was Phoebe Ann Moses, but everyone called her by her stage name, Annie Oakley.

"THIS LITTLE MISSIE"

Annie slopped through the mud alongside her husband, Frank Butler. Billed as the "Great Far West Rifle Shots," the couple worked for the Sells Brothers Circus, another outfit playing in New Orleans that winter. But the rain had dampened their act, too. Bored, looking to fill an afternoon, they had wandered over to the Wild West. With Bill as tour guide, they slipped into livestock tents where well-tended buffalo, ponies, and steers munched on fresh hay. They poked their heads into the cowboys' cozy tents and shook hands with American Indian performers. Everything they saw impressed them. So Frank asked for a job.

Bill turned them down. He already had plenty of shooting acts, including his own. Besides, the show was almost bankrupt. Who knew how much longer they could keep going? It simply wasn't a good time to hire a new act.

But Frank refused to take no for an answer. Confident that if Cody saw their act—and the audience's response to it—he'd want them in the show, Frank offered to give a few free performances.

Bill agreed. He invited them to join the Wild West at its next venue in Louisville, Kentucky.

Three weeks later, the couple arrived at the Louisville showground. While they waited to speak with Bill, Annie pulled out a gun and began practicing in the empty arena. Sighting with a hand mirror, she shot backward at the glass balls Frank tossed into the air. She hit them all.

At that moment a bearded man in a cutaway coat and bowler hat rushed forward. It was Nate Salsbury, back from his theater tour. And he knew a moneymaker when he saw one. He hired Annie on the spot.

He even spent thousands of precious dollars on posters, billboards, and advertisements to publicize her act. In Annie he saw more than a spectacular sharpshooter; he saw the answer to one of the Wild West's biggest problems. Up until now, the show's performers had all been men. Their acts—filled with manly skills such as roping, bronco riding, and shooting—were considered violent and destructive by many middle-class Americans. This, many people believed, made the show unsuitable for women and children.

Nate Salsbury, vice president of the Wild West, sitting before his tent on the show's encampment (c.1889).

Both Cody and Salsbury realized they were missing out on this much bigger audience. They knew the only way to draw in the middle class was to be considered a family entertainment. But how? They'd been stumped, until now.

Nate took one look at tiny, girlish, seemingly middle-class Annie firing her lethal weapons and knew he'd found the answer. She was, he realized, the perfect way to make gunplay appealing to respectable families.

Annie started work that very day. "I went right in and did my best before 17,000 people," she recalled.

Afterward, Cody introduced her to the other troupers. "This little missie here is Miss Annie Oakley," he told the men. "She's to be the only white woman with our show. And I want you boys to welcome her and protect her."

They did. "A crowned queen was never treated with more reverence than I was by those performers," Annie later said.

Billed as "The Peerless Wing and Rifle Shot," she received a special slot—first on the program after the Grand Entry. It was Bill's idea. "Her first shots brought forth a few screams of fright from the women, but they were soon lost in round after round of applause," recalled press agent Dexter Fellows. "It was she who set the audience at ease and prepared it for the continuous crack of firearms that followed."

The dainty, respectable-looking gunslinger soon entranced audiences. Not only were they impressed with her onstage shooting, but they heartily approved of her offstage behavior. From newspapers they learned that she loved doing needlepoint, designed and sewed her own costumes, served tea to guests who visited her showground tent, and adored dogs. Always, reported one newspaper, she acts in a "quiet and ladylike manner."

Her respectability rubbed off on the Wild West. People, including many middle-class families, came in droves. In Chicago alone, just weeks after Annie joined the troupe, forty thousand showgoers clamored for tickets. The same thing happened in Boston, Cleveland, and St. Louis. For the first time since soggy New Orleans, the Wild West was making money, big money. The show *would* go on.

Annie's popularity encouraged Bill to add more white women to the show. Over the years, hundreds of female shooters, ropers, and riders appeared in the Wild West. Among them were bronco-busting Lulu Belle Parr and Miss Victoria, who rode a white stallion around the arena before dismounting to swallow swords—some of them flaming! There were cowgirls Della and Bessie Ferrell, and Emma Lake Hickok, who'd learned her fancy riding from her legendary stepfather, Wild Bill Hickok.

There were also dozens of American Indian women in the Wild West, like Kitsipimi Otunna, a Sarcee actress who played the part of either a devastated "Indian maiden" whose husband had been killed in battle or a gracious "Indian interpreter" who helped Buffalo Bill communicate with "her people." Another was Plenty Shawls, an accomplished Lakota horseback rider and dancer.

Some people criticized the show's hiring of white women, saying their place was in the home. But Bill ignored them. "What we want to do is give our [white] women even *more* liberty than they have," he once explained. "Let them do any kind of work that they see fit, and if they do it as well as men, give them the same pay." After all, he added, it was "the square thing" to do.

Annie Oakley certainly earned a square salary. Soon she was making more money than any of the show's male stars—around $100 a week. (The American Indian women earned, on average, between $10 and $25 per week.)

But Annie wouldn't be the only unique attraction on the Wild West's program that season. In June 1885 one of the most famous men in America joined the troupe: Chief Sitting Bull.

ONE SEASON WITH SITTING BULL

After defeating Custer, Sitting Bull and his people had fled into Canada. From there the chief had watched as tribe after tribe lost the struggle to remain free. By 1881, almost all the Great Plains American Indians had been forced onto reservations. That same year, Sitting Bull and his band—starving, their hunting grounds depleted—had no choice but to join them. Surrendering to U.S. soldiers, Sitting Bull spent nineteen months imprisoned at Fort Randall before being allowed to live with his family and other Sioux at the Standing Rock Agency (or reservation) in the Dakota Territory.

Still, his noble spirit persisted. "Do you know who I am?" he once demanded of a visiting senator.

The senator certainly did. Dime novels and frontier-themed plays had fed the public's fascination with American Indian warriors. And since the Battle of the Little Bighorn, easterners were especially enthralled by Lakota warriors—Chiefs Crazy Horse, Rain-in-the-Face, Thunder Bear, Gall. But none was as famous as Sitting Bull.

Not long after Sitting Bull arrived at the Standing Rock Agency, Indian Agent James McLaughlin began organizing trips for him— some as far away as St. Paul and New York City. McLaughlin relished the idea of being Sitting Bull's "keeper," and he recognized the profit that could be made from the chief's public appearances. He also believed the trips would impress on the chief the importance of farming and getting a white man's education.

Sitting Bull was well aware of the agent's motives. Still, he welcomed these excursions. He knew white people would eagerly pay for his autograph, and he looked forward to earning some money. The Lakota have always endeavored to accumulate wealth, not for their personal use, but to give away to the needy. As a chief, custom dictated that Sitting Bull be generous with his tribe. These trips added to his reputation for benevolence.

There was another important reason for agreeing to travel. According to historian Jeffrey Means, Sitting Bull hoped to "establish a fictive kinship with some whites" while on these trips. That is, he wanted to create a "reciprocal relationship" that obligated officials in charge to "provide generously for the Lakota." It was yet another way the chief could look after his tribe.

And so, Sitting Bull laid the cornerstone of the newly designed capitol building in Bismarck. He toured factories, a school, and a fire department in St. Paul, and gave lectures to packed theaters in New York City. Wherever he went, curious crowds lined up to see him.

Bill desperately wanted the chief's crowd-drawing abilities. "I am going to try hard to get old Sitting Bull," he wrote. "If we can get him, our ever lasting fortune is made."

But Bill couldn't just offer the chief a job. That's because all Native people on reservations were considered wards of the federal government. Treated like children who needed control and direction, they were supervised in all aspects of their lives. This included employment. American Indians could not take a job unless the Bureau of Indian Affairs, headed by the secretary of the interior, granted permission.

So in April 1885, Bill wired the U.S. secretary of the interior, Lucius Lamar. "Please answer," he wrote, "as we are anxious for [Sitting Bull] to come at once."

But Lamar believed that jobs outside the reservations conflicted with the bureau's goal of "civilizing" American Indians, which meant requiring them to become as much like European Americans as possible: converting to Christianity, speaking English, farming an allotment of land, living in cabins rather than tipis, and wearing the clothes and hairstyles of white people. They most certainly should not, grumbled Lamar, be "roving through the country exhibiting themselves," and glorifying their "heathenish ways." And that applied as well to the famous Chief Sitting Bull. Picking up his pen, Lamar scrawled across the bottom of the telegram: "Make a *very* emphatic *No.*"

Bill persisted. He asked his old friends from his scouting days—General Philip Sheridan, the now-retired General William T. Sherman, and Eugene Carr, who now held the rank of colonel—for letters of recommendation. He then sent these endorsements to Lamar, along with his own letter promising to treat Sitting Bull well.

Impressed by Bill's important connections, Lamar gave in. In May, he granted permission for Sitting Bull, along with a few of the chief's family members and followers, to join the Wild West.

But Sitting Bull wasn't free to leave yet. The Bureau of Indian Affairs insisted that anyone hiring American Indians for Wild West shows, exhibitions, and other entertainments sign a contract promising to provide decent food, clothing, and medical care as well as a fair salary. The contract also required the hiring of a white male chaperone to keep tabs on the Native performers. The chaperone's name had to be submitted in advance for approval, along with his character references. Once approved, the chaperone was ordered to report under oath to a bureau official every two weeks describing the condition and behavior of the American Indians. Finally, the bureau contract stipulated that employers post a security bond of ten thousand dollars. Should the terms of the contract not be upheld, the bond was forfeited. Until Bill signed this contract, he could not take Sitting Bull—or any other American Indian—off the reservation.

Not until after the government granted its permission did anyone bother to ask the chief what *he* thought. Did Sitting Bull even want to join the show? Bill sent the show's general manager, John Burke, to convince him.

The two met at Sitting Bull's log cabin. Sitting by the front door, the chief looked out over the Grand River. From there he could see the spot where he'd been born. How drastically the world had changed. Years earlier he would never have chosen performing with the Wild

West over hunting in the traditional way on the Great Plains. But now? Once again, Sitting Bull saw the offer as an opportunity to earn some badly needed money for his tribe. Additionally, he saw it as a chance to meet with government policymakers, including the newly inaugurated president, Grover Cleveland. Hoping a change in presidents might mean a change for American Indians, he longed to talk with Cleveland about the problems on his reservation. The Wild West was his chance to get to Washington.

Turning to the general manager, Sitting Bull asked what was expected of him.

Not much, replied Burke. "Merely riding in the opening parade and appearing on the show grounds [is] enough."

Sitting Bull thought a moment, calculating. Then he demanded a salary of $50 a week (the average pay for a worker on the Pine Ridge Agency was $8 a month) and a $125 bonus. He also required $25 a month for each of the men accompanying him, and $15 for each of the three women. Additionally, he insisted on the right to keep all the money from sales of his pictures and autographs during the tour.

Burke agreed.

Days later, on June 12, 1885, Sitting Bull and his followers joined the show in Buffalo, New York. They arrived in the middle of a performance. They watched as Buffalo Bill shot glass balls from horseback and cowboys roped steers. Having finished her act, Annie Oakley went over to greet the famous chief. She had briefly met Sitting Bull a year earlier when he'd been in St. Paul. Now she asked if he remembered her.

The chief did. "I am very glad to see you," replied Sitting Bull through his interpreter. "I have not forgotten you, and feel pleased that you remember me."

Over the next few weeks as the show moved on—Detroit, Saginaw,

Grand Rapids—Sitting Bull, Annie claimed, "made a great pet of me." Exchanging gifts and photographs with her, he gave her a Lakota name and told her she should consider herself his adopted daughter. At the end of July, in a pipe-smoking ceremony, he also adopted Nate Salsbury. While neither Annie nor Nate took these adoptions seriously, Sitting Bull did. He was once again creating those "kinship relationships," although in Annie's case it was Sitting Bull who would have been the "generous provider and protector."

Sitting Bull exchanged gifts with Bill, too. And while his relationship with the showman wasn't as warm as the one he shared with Nate Salsbury, the chief apparently liked Buffalo Bill. He appreciated the respect with which Bill treated him. Instead of presenting him to audiences as Custer's killer, Bill introduced him as "The Renowned Sioux Chief, Sitting Bull." The chief held his head high as he rode among members of his tribe during the opening parade. And while the show's program still had a full-page illustration of Buffalo Bill scalping Yellow Hair, it also included a long article about Lakota religion in an attempt to teach audiences about Native cultures.

Proof that the two men respected each other can be found in a series of photographs they had taken together in Montreal. In them, Buffalo Bill and Sitting Bull appear almost as equals. But the most famous one, captioned "Foes in '76—Friends in '85," poses them in a way that, according to one historian, "speaks volumes." While both are shown in a dignified light, it is obvious that Bill is leading the way while Sitting Bull appears to be giving in. What was the subtext of the photo? That the "'friendship' offered in the photograph—and in Wild West performances—honored American Indian dignity only at the expense of surrender to white dominance and control."

This, of course, was the Wild West's narrative. Shaping their tale for their audiences, Bill and Nate consciously sold a triumphant story

This famous photograph of Sitting Bull and Buffalo Bill, titled "Enemies in '76, Friends in '85," was taken while the show toured Montreal. It is one of a series of eight poses showing the men standing before a painted backdrop in photographer William Notman's studio.

of western expansion and conquest. It was a story that needed both heroes and villains. Not surprisingly, American Indians were always assigned the role of the villains. Portrayed as savage warriors who stood in the way of virtuous Americans' westward movement, they were vanquished in show after show by the white hero played by Bill. Recalled one Native performer, "We take a great pleasure in going up against . . . the American soldiers even with blank cartridges." Then he shook his head in disgust. "But even then we don't get a square deal. We are always licked—always licked."

In the audience's mind, no one was more of a villain than Sitting Bull. Whenever he rode into the arena wearing his buckskin, paint, and feathers, audiences booed and hissed. He did not respond to these insults. Instead, he remained expressionless as he rode around the showground.

After his appearance, he returned to the tipi village, where he changed into his preferred clothes—flowered black pants, a printed shirt with tails hanging out, a red tie, and beaded moccasins. Despite their unfriendly behavior during the performance, showgoers flocked to his tipi. Eagerly, they bought up all kinds of Sitting Bull souvenirs—autographs, portrait photographs, and tobacco pouches. As for the pouches, he claimed each of these tiny buckskin bags had been personally used by him. In truth, he kept a large quantity of them on hand. Soon enough, the chief made money.

He gladly sent most of it home to his tribe. What remained he gave to beggars and ragged children he met on the street. He must have wondered what white people would do for American Indians if they cared so little about their own. "The white man knows how to make everything," he said, "but he does not know how to distribute it."

When the show traveled to Washington, D.C., Sitting Bull asked Bill to take him to the White House. He wanted to speak with President

An 1899 Wild West poster shows American Indians leading an attack against pioneers in covered wagons while the heroic-looking Bill is portrayed as the savior on horseback. It is a typical example of how Cody used his posters to present both the real and the mythic American West to audiences across the United States and Europe between 1883 and 1913.

Cleveland. While it's unclear if the two actually met, Sitting Bull did leave a letter for the president. Written with Bill's help, the chief's letter expressed his grave concerns about the living conditions on the reservation. He implored Cleveland to keep the government's promises to the American Indian.

Afterward, Bill and Sitting Bull strolled next door to army headquarters. General Sheridan was there, along with a delegation of fifteen other Native performers from the show. Amused by the paintings of western scenes that lined the parlor walls, the performers talked and laughed together. Occasionally, Sitting Bull spoke a few words to them. But he didn't utter a single word to Sheridan. Instead, he turned his back on the plump little general who'd done so much harm to his people.

While on tour, Sitting Bull also met Eugene Carr, now colonel of the Sixth Cavalry. The encounter, arranged by John Burke, took place in the sumptuous lobby of a St. Louis hotel. Seated on a velvet divan, Sitting Bull refused to stand when Carr approached. He did, however, take the general's outstretched hand. The two sat staring at one another. That's when Bill arrived with a group of reporters. Despite Carr's cordial greeting, a reporter for the *St. Louis Critic* noted a distinct coolness on the chief's part. His body language, the reporter wrote, "indicated he did not feel kindly toward the [colonel]."

Bill tried to convince the reporters that Sitting Bull was simply a man of few words. "[He] is too grave for newspaper correspondence," explained Cody. "He does not like a long interview."

And yet the chief gave lots of interviews. A favorite Wild West publicity gimmick was to host "frontier barbecues." At various cities, Bill and Nate asked dozens of reporters to lunch. Arriving on the showgrounds, the reporters followed the aroma of roasting meat past horse corrals and buffalo pens. Soon they spied cowboys turning big joints of oxen over open campfires. Sitting on the ground, visitors ate with a tin plate and a sharpened stick, just like on the frontier.

Afterward, they were led into a tent where they were given an interview with Sitting Bull. Taking a seat before them, the impassive chief waited for their questions with his interpreter at his side.

How did he like the East and its people? someone would always ask.

Sitting Bull gave the prepared answer: "They treat me very kindly. When I return to my people I shall tell them about our friends among the white men, and what I have seen."

Invariably, someone else asked about the Battle of the Little Bighorn. "[Did] he ever have any regret for his share in the Custer massacre?"

Usually Sitting Bull refused to answer this question. But once, his patience grown thin, he sprang to his feet. Thrusting a long, bony finger into the reporter's face, he growled to his interpreter, "Tell this fool that I did not murder Custer. It was a fight in open day. He would have killed me if he could. I have answered to my people for the dead on my side. Let Custer's friends answer for the dead on his side." Then he flung back the flap of his tent and stomped away.

By the time the show's season ended in October, Sitting Bull was tired of it all. "The wigwam is a better place for the Indian," he told a reporter after his final performance. "He is sick of the houses, and the noises and the multitudes of men. Sitting Bull longs for his wives and children. When he goes out the white men gather around him. They stare at him. They point fingers at him . . . Traveling is interesting and it pleases Sitting Bull, but the forest is better and his family pleases him more."

When he left, he took with him two gifts from Bill—a gray trick pony that he had ridden in the arena, and a white sombrero, size eight. He seemed to cherish them. One day when a relative wore the hat, Sitting Bull snatched it away. "My friend Long Hair gave me this hat. I value it very highly, for the hand that placed it on my head had a friendly feeling for me."

Sign-Up Days

Sitting Bull may have had enough, but hundreds of other American Indians followed him to the Wild West show. Although Bill hired Pawnee and Cheyenne, he preferred Lakota. Every spring—after applying to the secretary of the interior for permission to hire them—he would travel to the Lakota reservations looking for performers. These sign-up days became special events. Hundreds of people turned out. "Cody selected the lucky individuals himself," recalled one eyewitness. "The Indians . . . came in their finest buckskins, feathers, and beads. They were quite a sight . . . [but] only a small part [sixty or so] could be used, and the ones not chosen felt pretty bad about it."

Those hired were required to "play Indian," that is, meet white

This 1889 poster featuring Red Cloud plays into stereotypes held by many audience members that American Indians were cunning and wily tricksters. Red Cloud is a "Red Fox," states the poster. This was very intentional advertising. Cody intuited that the more "wild and bad" his Native performers were, the more alluring the show would be.

A panoramic view of Bill (center) with his Native performers (c. 1906).

audiences' stereotypical expectations of how American Indians should look and behave. Some members of the public found this practice repugnant. After all, Cody was asking his Native performers to reenact frontier battles, raids, and massacres in which they'd actually participated. Wasn't he exploiting the lives of these American Indians? Wasn't he manipulating and degrading these Native performers for his own advantage? "[He] is persistently perpetuating the [stereotype] that the Indian is only a savage being," declared a Brulé educator and lecturer named Chauncey Yellow Robe. Many Americans agreed. They believed that as guardians of the American Indians' physical and moral welfare, the federal government had an obligation to stop the Wild West's portrayal of their "heathenish ways." Hiring had to stop. American Indians needed protection from the likes of Buffalo Bill.

Cody responded by calling his critics "cranks." The government, he said, "wants to keep the Indians prisoners on their reservations and not allow them to earn an honest dollar." Didn't officials see that a life confined to poverty on the reservation did more harm than good? Besides, he argued, his Wild West show contributed to their education by "exposing them to the superiority of white culture and society." At that time, many people, including officials at the Bureau of Indian Affairs, believed Native Americans would be so dazzled by the white world outside their reservations that they would abandon their own culture in favor of it. If this was the case, wasn't Bill helping to compel American Indians to live and act like white men? The Wild West, he insisted, should be thanked, not condemned.

No matter how Bill replied to his critics, charges of exploitation and mistreatment continued to be leveled at the Wild West for the next thirty years. And yet American Indians still arrived in droves on sign-up days, the Bureau of Indian Affairs kept granting permission for them to be taken off the reservations, and Bill Cody continued to exhibit them. His show would have been lost without them.

⇢ PANNING FOR THE TRUTH ⇠
NATIVE PERFORMERS

Were the American Indians who appeared in Buffalo Bill's Wild West exploited? Did Bill use his Native performers to enhance his own reputation and make money? He certainly understood their draw. Over the show's long life, millions of people paid to see American Indians reenact historical events, demonstrate their equestrian skills, and perform dances. And Bill not only made a fortune but also became world famous. Neither would have happened without the American Indians. In the strictest sense, this *was* exploitation.

But as the Oglala scholar Vine Deloria Jr. points out, those who joined the Wild West—like Sitting Bull, American Horse, Black Elk, and No Neck—were not fools. They were not naïve, easily duped victims of Cody's trickery. Historian Louis Warren writes that they were "courageous men and women searching for a means of economic and cultural survival." And they flocked to join up with Buffalo Bill's Wild West. In the show's thirty-three-year run, over a thousand men, women, and children from various tribes traveled with it.

They had good reason. The U.S. government's so-called

Oglala Sioux chief American Horse and his wife (c. 1898). Because few portraits taken at the turn of the twentieth century caught the intimacy between Native performers and their wives, historians consider this an unusual and important portrait. American Horse joined the show in 1886. His wife went with him, remaining at his side for the next twenty years as he traveled and performed. During all that time, she not only tended to the family's needs but also supplemented their income by making beadwork and moccasins that she sold to showgoers.

civilizing policies were meant to extinguish the American Indians' traditional languages, cultures, and religions. Unable to leave reservations without a pass from the agent (the government's representative on the reservations), American Indians could not even visit relatives on another reservation without official permission. The core of the government's "Americanization" policy was to squeeze all nomadic tendencies out of tribes. They were compelled to live in log cabins (tipis were considered too traditional) and to take up farming or some other "meaningful labor" on the reservation.

That wasn't all. The government passed laws requiring American Indians to speak English. Traditional clothing was forbidden. No religious dances were allowed. No religious songs permitted. On Lakota reservations, sweat lodges—sacred structures for prayers and offerings—were dismantled. Instead, the people were expected to attend the reservations' Christian churches. Remarked one official, "I believe in immersing the Indian in our civilization, and when we get them under, holding them there until they are thoroughly soaked." He later added, "Kill the Indian, and save the man."

Joining the Wild West freed American Indians from the degrading confines of the reservation. For six months out of the year they once again lived tribally. The show's insistence on authenticity meant they could wear their traditional clothing, speak their traditional language, and live in traditional dwellings—all practices forbidden on the reservation. Since Bill did not restrict religious practices in his camp, sweat lodges popped up. Forbidden dances and songs were performed. Since a banned dance, if not performed, "will quickly fade from collective memory," claims historian Louis Warren, "it is not too much to say that social dances like the Omaha Dance and the Grass Dance were preserved partly through the Wild West."

The show also gave Native performers a chance to travel freely as a community. The Great Plains American Indians had always lived together in extended family groups or bands until U.S. policies forced them to separate. Performer George Dull Knife recalled that the show's tipi village "began to resemble camps [I] had always lived in on the Plains, with campfires, children running, women beading, men smoking and talking and occasionally fresh buffalo to eat, just like an Indian village."

Certainly, the American Indian performers were expected to re-create events from their recent past and "play Indian." But

some historians believe that many Native performers who remembered life before reservations saw this as a form of refusal
to abandon their culture. "Perhaps they realized in the deepest
sense," writes Vine Deloria Jr., "that even a caricature of their
youth was preferable to complete surrender to [Americaniza-
tion]." Or as Chief Black Heart once explained to a Bureau of
Indian Affairs official, "We were raised on horseback. That is
the way we had to work. [Buffalo Bill] furnished us the same
work we were raised for; that is the reason we want to work for
[him]."

Chief Iron Tail gets top billing in this 1912
poster. Bill knew that the Native
performers were the principal feature of
his show. In this instance the emphasis is
on Iron Tail as an individual. He is
portrayed with dignity.

Chief Iron Tail in a rare photograph of him
without his headdress and feathers (c. 1898).
A veteran of the Plains Wars, including the
Battle of the Little Bighorn, the Oglala chief
ended up traveling with the Wild West and
other shows for almost twenty years before
retiring in 1916. He was one of several
American Indians whose profile inspired the
face that appeared on the U.S. buffalo nickel
circulated at the beginning of the twentieth
century.

Oglala Sioux Rocky Bear (left) shown at his home at the Pine Ridge Agency with a mounted U.S. scout (c. 1891). Leader of and interpreter for the other Native performers, Rocky Bear took part in the tragedy-filled 1890 European tour. He was an outspoken supporter of the Wild West's treatment of American Indians.

There was another, more immediate reason: money. On the reservation, menial jobs such as chopping wood or driving a freight wagon paid less than eight dollars a month, and even those jobs were hard to find. But in Bill's show, the standard wage was twenty-five dollars a month—more if you were a chief or could translate languages. Bill liked to hire entire families (to retain the show's moral and family-oriented atmosphere), with wives receiving an additional ten dollars a month. This was a real windfall to Lakota families who were barely scraping by on the slim rations of food provided by the government. Many turned to performing to save themselves and their children from starvation.

Rocky Bear was one of them. When called before a group of bureau officials to explain why he'd joined up, he pointed out that the show fed him well. "That is why I am getting so fat." He touched his cheeks. "When I come back to the reservation I am getting poorer." If the "great father" in Washington forced him to give up the Wild West, he said, he would have no choice but to obey. But until then "this is the way I get my money." He then showed the officials his pockets, which were filled with three hundred dollars in gold coins. Everyone in the room knew he couldn't earn that kind of money on the reservation.

The bureaucrats lapsed into embarrassed silence.

WELCOME TO THE WILD WEST!

In June 1886, Buffalo Bill's Wild West set up camp for the summer on Staten Island, just a thirty-five-minute ferry ride across New York Bay from Manhattan. Advertising itself as "America's National Entertainment," the show drew New Yorkers in droves. Twice a day except Sunday, twenty thousand enthusiastic showgoers plunked down their fifty-cent admission (twenty-five cents for children) before jostling for seats in the steep canvas-covered grandstand that formed a horseshoe around the vast open-sky arena. The Cowboy Band burst into "The Star-Spangled Banner." Then a white canvas curtain at the far end of the showground opened. For the next two hours spectators sat glued to their seats as the western spectacle unfolded before them.

First up was Annie Oakley, followed by a horse race between a cowboy, a vaquero, and a Lakota man. After a reenactment of both the Pony Express and a wagon train crossing the prairie, Buck Taylor

The cowboys of the Wild West pose in front of the arena's painted backdrop (c. 1890). Unlike their real-life counterparts—rough ranch hands who were living hard—Cody insisted his cowboys be clean-cut heroes wearing Stetson hats and kindly smiles.

and his band of cowpokes moseyed into the arena for some "Cow-boy's Fun," a demonstration of roping and bronco riding. Next up? Buffalo Bill himself. Tall and handsome, with long dark hair and a dark goatee, the forty-year-old dashed into the arena on his milk-white stallion. One female showgoer gushed, "[He is] the most imposing man that America ever grew [with] a hint of border desperado lurking in his blazing eyes and a poetic fierceness in his features." He dazzled the crowd by blasting dozens of clay pigeons out of the sky as he rode at full gallop. As he charged back behind the curtain, the Deadwood stagecoach rumbled out. Within seconds the arena was a kaleidoscope of color and sound as a band of Lakota warriors rushed to attack the coach. Pistols fired. Horses whinnied. Men whooped and shouted. "There was enough firing of pistols to make the blood tingle and the children hide their heads," recalled one spectator.

Now it was Johnny Baker's turn. The sixteen-year-old had learned much from his foster father over the past three years, and had become a crack shot who could shatter clay pigeons while standing on his head. That season, a proud Buffalo Bill had given the teenager two gifts—a gold watch engraved to the "Champion Boy Shot of the World [from] his guardian William F. Cody" and his very own act. Johnny would remain a headliner in the show for the next forty years.

At this point, the show slowed its pace so that audience members could catch their breath. There were more races, as well as a demonstration of ceremonial dances presented by Native performers. At last—after a display of riding and roping by the Mexican vaqueros—came the eagerly awaited buffalo hunt. It was followed by the show's last act, the attack on a settler's cabin, an extravaganza of "men shooting from their saddles and riderless steeds dashing around." Then Bill gathered the entire cast in front of the grandstand for what the program called a "Salute," in which he dismissed the cast and invited the audience to visit the Wild West encampment before they headed home.

Located in a patch of woods on the water's edge, the encampment included the tipi village where men, women, and children from various tribes lived. Nearby, U.S. and foreign cavalrymen were housed in Sibley tents, while farther along a row of log cabins and adobe huts marked the residences of cowboys and vaqueros.

Visitors were encouraged to wander freely. "There were no

Bill liked to supervise the progress of his shows through a special peephole in the arena tent. He was quick to scold performers for what he considered run-of-the-mill performances and was constantly shouting, "Get the lead out of your britches!" This 1901 photograph shows him eyeballing the performance inside while behind him a group of American Indians await their cue.

restrictions," wrote one showgoer. "[We] are allowed to enter the tents, chuck the Indian babies under the chin, watch the [cowboys] at work or interview the . . . chiefs."

Even Bill's tent was open to the public. The biggest of them all, it was furnished with buffalo rugs covering the dirt floor, knickknacks on tabletops, and comfortable chairs. There were no saddles flung in the corners or guns hanging on the walls. There wasn't even a pistol peeking from the showman's pocket, just the wire-rimmed glasses he used for reading. Still, his tent was one of the most popular attractions. Day after day crowds of parents huddled around his door. They asked only that their children be allowed to shake hands with him, and Buffalo Bill always agreed.

This postcard from the 1905 Paris exhibition shows the vast layout of the Wild West. To the left of the huge horseshoe-shaped arena is the big dining tent. The pointed tops of tipis in the encampment's "Indian Village" can be seen toward the picture's middle, while other performers' tents are scattered throughout the park's newly planted trees.

Visitors were awed by the size of the encampment. Taking up an area of two city blocks, it consisted of 140 tents (not counting the grandstand),

A group of Native performers pose in front of their tipis in their encampment at Erastina in Staten Island, New York (c. 1886).

stables enough for eight hundred animals, a huge dining tent complete with kitchen, and a post office. There was even a park complete with shrubs, trees, and paved walkways created by show workers just for the Staten Island engagement.

More than five hundred people traveled with the show. Besides the performers, there were butchers, bakers, pastry chefs, and a kitchen full of cooks. There were waiters and dishwashers, laundrymen and firemen. Blacksmiths kept the horses shod; grooms and stable boys kept them clean and fed. Manual laborers included leatherworkers, wheelwrights, carpenters, tent men, and mechanics; service workers included ticket sellers, bookkeepers, money counters, and a horde of publicists. In one tent, confectioners whipped up the show's signature refreshment: pink-and-white popcorn balls.

All summer long, stories about the Wild West appeared in New York's newspapers. One morning, readers learned that Bill "could ride with a cup of water on his head and not spill a drop." Another morning, they read that Nate Salsbury had treated the Native performers to a feast of five hundred pies. What kind? The newspapers merely called them "Yankee pies." The performers, they noted, devoured them with delight.

And one July morning readers opened their newspapers to find a generous invitation. Buffalo Bill promised to give a free ticket to every newsboy or bootblack riding to Staten Island on the first boat on a certain day. Remembering what it was like to be a poor working boy, he wanted to give them a special treat.

Fifteen hundred boys stormed the showground that day. Each was given a sack lunch and seated in a special reserved section of the grandstand. According to one newspaper, the boys "yelled and clapped with such force it seemed as though they shook the island." When the show ended, Cody rode over to speak just with them. He urged the boys to go to school and become good citizens. And in later years, no matter where they saw him, he wanted them to come up and tell him what they'd accomplished. The boys promised they would. For the rest of the summer, whenever Bill walked down New York's streets, gangs of idolizing boys tagged along behind, pushing free newspapers or shoe shines on him.

Stories like these kept crowds lined up at the Wild West ticket booth. By summer's end, the show had played to more than one million people—roughly the entire population of New York City.

People came more than once. General Sherman saw it twenty times. The author Mark Twain came two days in a row. Even P. T. Barnum— the most famous showman of his day—took in a performance. Hobbling on crutches, his foot wrapped in bandages because of severe gout, the seventy-six-year-old circus owner had never before gone to see a show other than his own. He liked what he saw. Speaking with

Nate Salsbury afterward, Barnum suggested the partners take the Wild West to Europe.

Bill and Nate took the showman's advice. Months later, on March 31, 1887, Buffalo Bill's Wild West sailed out of New York Harbor. It was bound for England—and international fame.

Cossacks lead the charge into the arena (c. 1896).

ACT

SEVEN

ROUGH RIDERS OF THE WORLD
OR
"COSSACKS OF THE CAUCASUS OF RUSSIA, IN FEATS OF HORSEMANSHIP, NATIVE DANCES ETC."

—Buffalo Bill's Wild West Program, 1894

A SCENE FROM THE WILD WEST

A peculiar horde of horsemen race into the arena. They wear high conical hats, knee-length belted coats crisscrossed with ammunition sashes, and tall leather boots sporting sharp silver spurs. Showgoers lean forward. These are not "Howdy, ma'am" cowboys. These are dark-bearded Russian Cossacks. They look exotic, ferocious, different. But are they better riders than the Americans?

"The great interest which attaches itself to the whole show is that it enables the audience to take sides on the question of which [nation of] people ride best," noted one spectator.

The Cossacks astonish.

Performing at lightning speed, the horses at full gallop, the Cossacks stand on their heads in the saddle. The audience barely has time to gasp before they switch positions.

They dangle off the sides of their saddles until their heads—mere inches from the horses' pounding hooves—brush the ground.

They vault on and off their charging steeds.

They somersault over hindquarters and ride upside down, clinging to their horses' bellies.

The audience has never seen anything like it.

The Cossacks leap onto their horses' backs. Standing impossibly tall and straight in the jouncing saddles, they pull out great curved swords. Their expressions fierce and warlike, they slash at the air with powerful strokes as they thunder around the arena.

The sight sends a shiver up many a showgoer's spine. Is it any wonder the program calls them "graduates from [the] fierce school of sabre and saddle"? And yet, for all the Cossacks' acrobatic skill, most in the audience agree that the American cowboy is still the better horseman. He has something extra on his side—"grace of carriage, an easy seat in the saddle, a courageous bearing." In their minds, a contest between the Old World and the New has just taken place. And to their enormous satisfaction, the New World has won. Pleased, showgoers settle back into their seats as the horsemen leave the arena.

SEA-TOSSED SHOW

The ship carrying Buffalo Bill's Wild West tossed on the rough Atlantic seas. In the dingy hold below, the show animals bellowed for fresh air. Taking pity on them, the ship's captain ordered holes cut in the deck. The ventilation improved, but not before one of the horses died. Crew members tossed its body overboard.

The people on board were equally miserable. In their bunks in steerage, the newly hired American Indians—among them Spotted Eagle, Rushing Bear, and the star of the Lakota contingent, Chief Red Shirt—pinched themselves to see if they were wasting away. They believed that crossing the ocean would cause their flesh to decay and fall off their bones. Now and then, they sang their death songs.

Bill could offer little comfort. The rolling waves had made him

The cast of the Wild West gathered on the deck of the *State of Nebraska* for this photograph of their journey to England in 1887. Bill is, as usual, front and center.

"sick as a cow with a hollow horn." Only Annie Oakley escaped sea-sickness. She delivered cups of tea to the ailing troupers, along with assurances that the rough sea would soon pass.

On the third day out, it did. The ship sailed smoothly on to England.

Londoners awaited it eagerly. For weeks the city had been plastered with colorful posters showing American Indians attacking a stage-coach and cowboys lassoing mustangs. Now, as the ship moved up the Thames River and into the Gravesend docks that April day in 1887, an excited crowd gathered on the wharf. They hoped for a glimpse of the Wild West.

They were not disappointed. On the ship's upper deck stood the American Indians in full ceremonial regalia—Mr. and Mrs. Eagle Horse, Rushing Bear, Tall Medicine, to name a few. Buffalo Bill walked among them, his long hair waving in the wind. At his side glinted a jeweled sword that had been given to him by some army officers just before he'd set sail. They had also conferred on him the rank of "colonel." It was meant merely as an honorary title, but Bill seized on it. Now he proudly called himself Colonel Cody. He insisted others do so too.

After a brief quarantine on board, the steam winch whirred and the crates holding buffalo, elk, and deer swung out of the holds. The crowd cheered, and the Cowboy Band struck up "Yankee Doodle Dandy." Then the entire cast—Mexican vaqueros, lady riders, sharpshooters (including Johnny Baker), and more—streamed down the gangway. Boarding a waiting train, they rode the twelve miles to Earls Court, where the Wild West would be playing all summer long.

The ground at Earls Court had already been smoothed and graded, and a fence encircled all seven acres of the showground. A covered horseshoe-shaped grandstand big enough to hold twenty-five thousand was going up, as well as stables and corrals. Optimistically, the partners had also ordered the construction of a royal viewing box. With any luck, they'd soon be filling it with Europe's blue bloods.

All the troupers, even Bill, pitched in, unloading the train quickly. By nightfall, the animals were stabled and tipis and tents sprouted in a grove of newly planted trees. It was "a canvas city," remarked Bill, ". . . sprung up in the West End of London." All it needed was one last touch—the American flag. With the Cowboy Band playing "The Star-Spangled Banner," the Stars and Stripes were raised. As the song's last notes faded, "a storm of shouts and cheers . . . [rose] from the thousands that lined the walls, streets and housetops of the surrounding neighborhoods," recalled Bill. Since the dining tent wasn't up yet, the curious crowd watched the performers eat at long tables in the open air. Then, one by one, the exhausted travelers headed to their tents to sleep for the first time on English soil.

LASSOING LONDON

Stage fright. For the first time in years, Bill had a bad case of stage fright. What, he must have asked himself, were he and Nate thinking when they'd invited Prince Albert Edward—Queen Victoria's oldest son, later to become King Edward VII—to an advance performance of the show? They weren't ready for such illustrious visitors. The performers had barely rehearsed. And the grounds were rutted and swampy from the rainy weather. Still, it was a golden opportunity. A visit from the prince was guaranteed to generate lots of good publicity, *if* everything went off without a hitch.

On May 5, the short, pudgy prince arrived with his wife, Alexandra, and their daughters, Louise, Maud, and Victoria. A large party of England's upper crust trailed them—lords and ladies, dukes and earls. Nerves jangling, Bill led the group to the royal box. But he couldn't stay. He was just too tense. Leaving Nate to explain the acts, he hurried off to watch the show from the wings.

Bill's worries evaporated the moment the canvas curtain was drawn back. Out galloped the Lakota warriors, yelling and sweeping around the arena like a whirlwind. The effect on the royal guests, claimed Bill, "was electric." The prince stood and leaned eagerly over the front of the box, while the others thrilled at the spectacle.

"Cody, you've fetched 'em," Bill congratulated himself.

He had, indeed. At show's end the party even tramped through the mud to visit the encampment. They wandered through the tipi village and rested at Cody's tent. Then the prince asked to see the show's stables. An avid outdoorsman, he was impressed by the "apple pie order" of the place. And he endeared himself to Bill when he stopped at the stall belonging to Bill's twenty-one-year-old stallion, Charlie. Stroking the horse's nose, he asked to hear the animal's history.

"My old horse . . . has carried me through many dangers many times," bragged Bill. "[He] once bore me in a flight of 100 miles in nine hours, forty minutes when chased by a band of hostile Indians."

As if verifying the story, Charlie nickered.

By the next morning, all of England knew about the Prince of

Bill sits astride his beloved old horse Charlie in 1887.

Wales's visit. "The Wild West is upon every tongue," reported the *London Daily Chronicle*. Cody mania swept the city. Four days later, the show opened to thunderous applause. "It is new, it is brilliant, it will 'go,'" proclaimed one British magazine.

Go, it did. Londoners flocked to the grandstand. "The crush and fight, the struggle amongst both quadrupeds and bipeds to reach the gates of the [Wild West] was, for some hours, something terrific," the *Evening News* reported. Carriages jammed the roads leading to the arena, and the sidewalks were "just as bad." Each afternoon, thousands showed up hours before the performance to make sure they got a seat. Each afternoon, thousands more were turned away. "Sold out," read the sign in the ticket window. In May alone, the Wild West played to half a million people.

The show was the talk of the city. Tongues wagged about the cowboys and American Indians who turned up one day at Westminster

Abbey. Another day, they appeared at the Congregational Chapel in West Kensington, where the Lakota astonished churchgoers by singing the hymn "Nearer My God to Thee." One Tuesday night Chief Red Shirt, Buck Taylor, and some others went to a play at the Lyceum Theatre. Seated in a private box and munching on sweet plums, they watched the performance. Afterward, reporters asked what they thought.

Red Shirt answered that it all seemed like a dream.

Buck Taylor didn't answer at all. He just sat there like a rock.

But the most popular Wild West performer remained Buffalo Bill himself. Admired by most Londoners for his "coal black eyes . . . flowing hair [and] most splendid moustache," the showman appeared "manly and imposing, yet speaks with a kind, gentle voice and has a smile as sweet as a woman's." When out of the arena, he exchanged his buckskins for dark tweed suits and shirts with diamond-studded cuff links. "Everyone is of the opinion that he is altogether the handsomest man they have ever seen," gushed one lady.

Invitations poured in—breakfasts, luncheons, dinners, garden parties, midnight dances, soirees, musicals. Bill was made an honorary member of London's most fashionable clubs. He frequented the country homes of the rich and famous. And he dined at the House of Commons, where he charmed his tablemates with his amusing stories.

This social schedule combined with his workload kept him busy eighteen hours a day. "It's pretty hard work with two and three performances a day and the society racket, receptions, dinners etc.," he wrote a friend. Still, he reckoned it was worth it. "With my European reputation, you can easily guess the business I will do when I get back to my own country."

News of his social successes made its way back to America. In North Platte, folks were astounded by the reports. Wrote one newspaper editor, "A few years ago W. F. Cody was shooting buffalo and dodging Indians . . . and drinking bad whiskey in western Kansas. Then everybody called him 'Buffalo Bill.' Now he is the social lion in London and Lords and Ladies are running over each other to get an introduction to him and call him 'Colonel . . .' There is nothing [more incredible] than this in any romance."

But things were about to get even more incredible.

"GRANDMOTHER ENGLAND"

In her private rooms at Windsor Castle, Queen Victoria overheard snatches of conversation about the Americans' big western show. Intrigued, she called for her son. What did he think about it?

Prince Albert Edward couldn't hide his enthusiasm. He told her about the Deadwood stagecoach and the attack on the settler's cabin, about Annie Oakley and Chief Red Shirt and Buffalo Bill. Really, she *must* see it for herself.

How? The queen rarely appeared in public. For twenty-six years, since her husband's death in 1861, she had remained mostly in seclusion. But now her curiosity was whetted. She commanded Buffalo Bill and his troupe to give a private performance at the palace.

Impossible, replied Bill. The show was too big for Windsor Castle. Did Her Majesty really think it was a good idea to have so many animals running around the palace? If she wanted to see it, she would just have to come to the arena.

Astonishingly, she agreed.

The next afternoon, the queen's closed carriage rattled down the street toward Earls Court. Along the route, crowds cheered her return to public life. It had been so long since she had ridden among them. Some subjects, however, were insulted. Why had Her Majesty graced the Wild West with her presence "but never since her husband's death has she set foot . . . in an English show place?" sniffed one Londoner. It seemed Buffalo Bill could lure *everyone* to his show.

The carriage rattled through the show's gates, entered the arena, and drove to the royal box. Dressed in black silk with white lace cuffs and matching cap, the queen swept regally to her seat. With her came a dozen other royals, as well as her military attendants and ladies-in-waiting. Victoria gave the signal to begin.

"Indians . . . cowboys, Mexicans . . . all came tearing round at full speed, shrieking and screaming which had the weirdest effect," Victoria wrote in her diary that night. "An attack on a coach & on a ranch, with an immense deal of firing, which was most exciting, so was the buffalo hunt and the bucking ponies."

Afterward, the queen favored many of the performers with handshakes and compliments. Both Bill and Chief Red Shirt were presented to her, as were the "American girls" Annie Oakley and Lillian Smith. Then Black Elk, a young Oglala, and some others were asked to dance for "Grandmother England," as he called the queen. When

This engraving, which appeared in the May 1887 edition of *The Graph*, an English publication, shows Buffalo Bill and a handful of Native performers welcoming Queen Victoria (seated far left) to the Wild West show.

they finished, she said, "I have seen all kinds of people; but today I have seen the best looking people I know." Then she shook hands with the dancers. Recalled Black Elk, "Her hand was very little and soft. We gave a big cheer for her and then the shining wagons came in and she got into one of them and they all went away."

A Sad Event at Sea

Two appearances a day. Six days a week. For six months. By the time the Wild West gave its final London performance on October 31, 1887, Bill Cody was longing for home. He pined for his ranch and the fresh Nebraska air. "We are doing an immense business here," he admitted, "but the country cramps me and the climate chokes me. There is not air enough . . . I want to come home."

Bill had to wait. Packing up, the show headed for other English cities—Birmingham first, followed by Manchester. Hundreds more performances. Six more months. But at last, the Wild West bade farewell to England. After more than a year, it sailed for home.

Halfway to America, tragedy struck. One morning, Bill went down into the hold to visit Charlie as he always did. The showman stroked the horse's velvety nose, whispered in his ear, and gave him a cube of sugar. "He seemed to be as well as usual," said Bill.

Hours later Charlie's groom hurried to the upper deck. The horse, he told Bill, was sick.

Bill rushed back to the hold. The horse had a chill. He coughed. And when the showman pressed his ear to Charlie's chest, he could hear crackles and wheezes. "Lung fever," Bill diagnosed. Rarely leaving his old friend's side, he tended him with herbal concoctions and flannel poultices. Nothing worked. In the early morning hours of the third day, Charlie died. Lamented Bill, "We could almost understand each other and I felt very deeply."

He asked some sailors to stitch up the horse's body into a canvas shroud. Then they lifted it to the upper deck and draped it with an American flag. There the horse's body lay in state. For the rest of the day crew members and troupers filed past to pay their respects.

When the setting sun at last cast its pink and gold rays across the deck, the entire ship's company gathered. The Cowboy Band played

Taken just three years after he left Fort McPherson, this 1876 photo shows Bill Cody looking more like a gentleman than a frontiersman.

"Auld Lang Syne." Performers lit candles. And the sailors gently lowered the body of the faithful friend into the water. Eyes moist, Bill watched until it sank from view. Then the ship's cannon boomed a final farewell. Charlie was gone.

"HERO OF TWO CONTINENTS"

Six days later, the ship steamed into New York Harbor. Crowds cheered. Flags waved. Bands played. Bill had left the country a local celebrity, but he returned an international star. The "Hero of Two Continents," as the *New York Evening Telegram* put it, "had come home."

But the hero had changed. No longer did he sleep in a tent on the showground. Now he lived in a suite at the Waldorf-Astoria, the city's swankiest hotel, where he held almost nightly soirees with New York's upper crust. Dressed in a tailored suit and tie, he patronized the most upscale restaurants. Only in the arena was there any remnant left of Buffalo Bill the plainsman.

No matter. Audiences lauded him as the man who had made

American culture popular in Europe. This was no small feat. European critics constantly turned up their noses at American art, music, fashion, theater, and literature. Explained one British pundit, "Nothing very original, nothing pointedly national, has ever come from [the United States]." So imagine Americans' pride when they heard reports of Buffalo Bill's triumphs in England. Wrote one fan, "The presence of the Queen . . . the Prince, and the British public are marks of favor which reflect back on America." American entertainment had been validated as bona fide culture. The country was just as good as—maybe better than—European nations. And who did they have to thank for it? Buffalo Bill Cody. Their gratitude spilled over into lionizing interviews, rave reviews, and, above all, ticket sales.

Once again, the Wild West pitched camp on Staten Island. The booking was only for the month of June. But the opening-day crowd of twenty thousand on May 31, 1888, with another ten thousand lined up at the gates unable to get in, convinced Bill to remain until mid-August. Besides, he was enjoying his wild popularity. That summer the *New York World* described him as the "best known man in New York City. Wherever he goes he is recognized and pointed out in crowds." Children followed him in the streets, and women gaped when he walked by. As one historian put it, "The man of the year was William F. Cody."

HARD LIVING WITH LULU

Two years and seven months. That's how long Bill had been away from North Platte. But now on this gray day in November 1888 he was steaming across the wide-open Nebraska prairie. As his train passed Scout's Rest Ranch, he proudly noted the sturdy growth of the young fruit trees his brother-in-law Al Goodman had recently planted. Al and Julia managed the place for him now, along with their five sons and two daughters. From the ranch's tidy appearance, Bill knew they were doing a fine job.

Two miles farther on, the train glided into the North Platte station. On the platform waited an enthusiastic welcoming party. Peering out the window, Bill scanned their faces. Lulu's wasn't among them. He must have sighed with relief. He hadn't seen his wife in all the time he'd been away. And he hadn't written her since before sailing for London. Not one word.

She'd responded with like silence.

Twenty-two-year-old Arta tried to get her parents to make up. "I would give anything if our home was bright and cheerful," she wrote her father. "Do not blame or feel angry toward dear mamma . . . Do not say, dear papa, that you will go to Europe and never return, for that is not right."

Little did Arta know that arrangements had already been made for a tour of continental Europe. The Wild West would sail in four months. Meanwhile, Bill hoped to get some rest out at the ranch. He and Lulu still kept separate homes in North Platte, so escaping from her bad humor wasn't entirely impossible. Still, he'd be expected to spend most of his time with his family at their house in town. And then there were all those social events folks had planned in his honor. He and Lulu had no choice but to go as a couple.

Bill straightened his broad shoulders. It would just have to be faced.

Alighting from the train, he was greeted with plenty of back thumping and handshaking. Then the townsmen swept their most illustrious citizen across the street to Laing's Saloon. Bill went along agreeably. Now that the show was closed for the winter, he wouldn't be breaking his promise to Nate Salsbury not to drink during the touring season. Besides, he needed some liquid courage before facing Lulu.

Over at the Welcome Wigwam, Lulu had the flag run up the tall pole in her front yard. This was a signal to their friends that Bill was in town. Those who hadn't been to the station would be glad to know he'd finally arrived.

Lulu was glad, too. She'd missed her husband. More than anything she longed to be with him, and his long absences left her feeling sad and unloved. Unfortunately, those feelings found expression in angry outbursts. Whenever she was with her husband, she criticized, nagged, and complained. Above all, she expressed jealousy.

And with good reason. She knew about the relationship he'd struck up with a Kentucky widow named Mollie Moses. Mollie had attended the Wild West when it played near her hometown. Afterward, she'd gone around to Bill's tent and introduced herself. He, in turn, asked her to dinner. When the show moved on, the two continued to write to each other. Romance blossomed.

At first, Bill told Mollie he was single. But when she pressed him on the subject, he backpedaled. "My wife and I have separated, but no divorce yet," he tried to explain. "That's what I meant by saying . . . I am a single man."

Later, he asked Mollie to wait for him in St. Louis. "Go to the St. James Hotel if I ain't there to meet you," he wrote. "I got you the white horse, and a fine saddle. Suppose you have your [riding clothes]."

Did Mollie go? It's unclear.

But the affair pained Lulu deeply. No wonder she constantly questioned his faithfulness. Were there others?

Most certainly. Rumors from England had reached Lulu's ears about a beautiful American actress named Katherine Clemmons. Clemmons had frequently been seen with Bill, who reportedly called her "the finest looking woman in the world." When Lulu heard that, she seethed.

The minute Bill stepped into the parlor she flew at him. What would his hero-worshipping audience think if she went public with his dalliances? she demanded. It would ruin his family-man image. Did he want that?

They argued about money, too. Despite all he'd earned in England, Bill was strapped for cash. Reluctant to mortgage any part of his beloved ranch, he had decided instead to mortgage some of his other North Platte property. This was necessary in order to raise enough for the upcoming European tour. But because Lulu had put this property in her name, he needed her signature to do it.

She refused.

Bill later groused, "If only Lulu would help me a little I could tide over like a flirt, but she won't sign her name to anything."

Her husband saw her actions as betrayal. But Lulu believed she was protecting herself and their two remaining children from a spendthrift who might risk everything they owned to fund a theatrical performance or some other moneymaking scheme.

Money did slip through Bill's fingers like water. Certainly, he'd invested in his ranch and other North Platte properties. But he'd also sunk a lot of cash into schemes that never panned out—patent medicines, a printing plant, and a cereal company. Friends and family further drained his bank account. Not only did he still support his sisters and their families, but he paid off the mortgages of five North Platte churches, gave every saloonkeeper in town a fine gold watch and chain, and bought uniforms for both the North Platte town band and the girls' drill team. "Send the bill to Buffalo Bill," he liked to say.

No wonder Lulu stood firm with regard to the North Platte property.

Still, to North Platte's citizens that winter, Mr. and Mrs. Cody seemed to get along just fine. They attended receptions, dinners, and plays. They held a banquet in honor of Wyoming's governor, and they traveled to Lincoln to attend the inauguration of Nebraska's governor.

But those closest to the couple knew better.

Late one night Bill arrived at the ranch. He pounded on the Goodmans' door. "Are you awake?" he shouted. "Get up, come out here and talk."

Sleepily, Julia and Al let him in.

Disheveled, his eyes red and swollen from crying, he wailed, "How can I stand it? I can't stay over there in peace with her. I want you to tell me what to do. It is more than I can stand . . ."

"Willie, it will soon blow over," comforted Julia. "Never mind."

Bill wasn't so sure.

To calm him, Al took him for a carriage ride. The icy temperature must have had a bracing effect. Bill slept at the ranch that night. But the next morning, he returned to his wife and daughters. After all, he didn't have to put up with Lulu too much longer. He'd be leaving for Europe soon.

The Wild West could bridge cultures, as this 1911 photograph of a white boy sharing food with an unidentified American Indian girl shows. The boy was visiting the encampment's tipi village.

TRIUMPH IN PARIS

The Wild West opened at the World's Fair in Paris, France, on May 19, 1889. Parisians thrilled to it. Twice each day, fifteen thousand spectators packed the grandstand while thousands more were turned away. Bill, whom the French had idolizingly dubbed "the Napoleon of the prairie," was amused to see that "fashionable young men bought American . . . saddles for their rides in the Bois. Cowboy hats appeared everywhere on the streets. Relics from the plains and mountains, bows, moccasins and Indian baskets sold like hot cakes in the souvenir stores."

Before and after the show, French citizens flocked to the Wild West encampment, where they lingered in the tipi village. "[The performers] are already a chic attraction," noted the *New York Times*, and the "warriors are courted and feted by the prettiest women in Paris." Indeed, within weeks of the show's opening one of the Wild West's Native performers ran off with a French noblewoman. The couple planned on buying a ranch and settling in British Canada.

Annie Oakley also held court for her French fans. They showered her with gifts. Two sets of silverware, a solid-silver teapot, and antique sugar bowls already covered the table in her tent. And even though she was already married, the sharpshooter received four marriage proposals, too, including one from a French count. "I shot a bullet through the head of [his] photograph," she later told a reporter, "and mailed it back with 'respectfully declined' on it."

As for Bill, he was back to the busy social life. This time he fielded invitations from the president of France, the shah of Persia, and the former queen Isabella II of Spain.

But the most interesting request came from the celebrated French artist Rosa Bonheur. She arrived at the encampment on a chilly morning in September. Stepping from her carriage, she looked around in wonder at the grazing buffalo, the tents and tipis. Bill took her on a tour, then invited her into his tent for lunch. As they settled into comfortable chairs, Bonheur asked a favor. Would Bill allow her to become an artist-in-residence at the camp?

How could he deny such a famous artist? Besides, he liked the gray-haired woman with the penetrating blue eyes. He agreed.

After that, Bonheur rode out to the showground most mornings. Strolling about the tipi village, she would search for a scene that sparked her. "Observing [the people] at close range really refreshed my sad old mind," she said.

BUFFALO BILL ON HORSEBACK.
From the Famous Painting by Rosa Bonheur.

The painting by Rosa Bonheur that Bill hung proudly in his North Platte parlor.

Red Shirt and Rocky Bear posed for Bonheur, as did other Wild West performers. Her many sketches resulted in seventeen paintings, some of chiefs riding or hunting, others of families outside their tipis. One was of Bill himself, wearing buckskin and thigh-high boots, trotting along on a white horse. She gave it to him as a gift.

Bill loved it. Shipping it home to North Platte, he asked that it be hung on his parlor wall next to the portrait of Kit.

TRAGEDY ON TOUR

After closing in Paris in early October, the Wild West swung through the south of France, then headed to Barcelona, Spain. Here, bad luck struck. A flu epidemic swept through the city, ravaging its citizens. Almost half the company fell ill, including Annie and the show's announcer, Frank Richmond. Annie recovered, but Richmond died. As soon as city officials lifted the quarantine, Nate Salsbury—eager to quit the place—booked the first steamer out.

The show fled to Naples, Italy. Here troupers convalesced in the warm sun. But they hadn't escaped bad times. Local outbreaks of smallpox and typhoid carried off Featherman, Goes Flying, and Chief Hawick (Swift Hawk). Another Native performer, Little Ring, was found dead in his bed, apparently from a bad heart.

Despite these tragedies, the show went on, to Florence, Bologna, Milan, Verona, and Venice. In Rome in early March, special arrangements were made for Bill and a small group of Lakota to attend the twelfth anniversary of Pope Leo XIII's coronation. Dressed in their traditional beaded buckskin and moccasins (Bill wore a dress coat), they waited in the Ducal Hall for His Holiness to pass on his way to the Sistine Chapel for a special mass marking the occasion.

In swept the pope, his robes flowing. As he passed the Wild West contingent, Rocky Bear, who'd attended classes taught by Catholic missionaries at the Pine Ridge Agency, knelt and made the sign of the cross. The pope slowed. Leaning forward, he blessed the group. "He seemed genuinely moved by the Chief's gesture," recalled one eyewitness.

The group remained solemn until the pope was gone. Then they burst into laughter. They found the guards with their feathered helmets and heavy two-handed swords ridiculous. "Such gaudy warriors could have been dropped by arrows or shot from a treasured Winchester before they could heft such blades over their heads," one guffawed.

SUSPICIONS, ALLEGATIONS, AND INVESTIGATIONS

Days later, a reporter asked Rocky Bear what he thought of Europe. "The more I see of other countries, the more I like America," Rocky Bear replied. Among his complaints? "Everyone hold his hand out for money here . . . [and] there are too many soldiers." Especially galling was the way Italians laughed at him. This had not been the case in England or France. But in Italy, people jeered and pointed whenever the Native performers walked along the streets. "We will all be very glad to go home," Rocky Bear concluded.

Tired of touring, Red Shirt and his family had already sailed home. Now five more Lakota headed for America, including Kills Plenty, whose arm had been crushed when a horse fell on him. A few days after he arrived in New York, however, he died from blood poisoning. Reporters grew suspicious. There were so many recent deaths. Was Buffalo Bill mistreating his Native performers?

Bill knew officials at the Bureau of Indian Affairs were watching closely. Its new commissioner, Thomas Jefferson Morgan, believed his mission was to force Native people to "conform to the white man's ways." He had longed to put an end to American Indian performances promoting what he considered savagery and the old way of life. Now he pointed to the deaths as proof that American Indians should not take part in such shows.

Meanwhile, the Wild West moved on to Germany. Here it enjoyed both sold-out shows and lavish gifts from the local aristocracy. Annie even added a diamond bracelet from a Bavarian count to her already overflowing gift collection. It appeared good luck had returned to the show. Bill and Nate were confident the controversy would soon blow over.

Then tragedy struck again. An Oglala named Wounds One Another was killed when he accidentally fell from a moving train. Weeks later, Uses the Sword slipped off his horse during a performance. Before the audience's horrified eyes, he was trampled to death by a buffalo.

Seven deaths. It was too many. Officials called for a formal investigation into Cody's treatment of the American Indians in his employ. Until it was completed, the Wild West was banned from hiring any more Native performers.

In Germany, the partners grew genuinely alarmed. Without Native performers there would be no show. Nate Salsbury and John Burke, the show's general manager, immediately departed for America to fight the new ruling. With them went the remaining seventy-nine Native performers. All were in good condition, proof that none had been mistreated.

Meanwhile, Bill finished settling the show into winter quarters near Strasbourg, Germany. Then, leaving twenty-one-year-old Johnny Baker in charge, he, too, caught a ship bound for America. After all, who better to plead their case than the hero of two continents? As his ship steamed across the sea, Cody paced the deck impatiently.

He hoped Salsbury and Burke could handle the situation until he arrived.

On November 13, 1890, the ship carrying Salsbury, Burke, and the performers sailed into Philadelphia. It had barely docked before a swarm of waiting reporters began shouting questions. Were the allegations true? Did Buffalo Bill mistreat his Native performers?

Three officials from the Bureau of Indian Affairs also waited on the dock. The minute the ship tied up, the men bolted up the gangway.

The reporters followed.

Burke met them all on deck. For the benefit of the note-taking newspapermen, he loudly denounced the officials as "notoriety-seeking busybodies" who "without rhyme, truth or reason have tried to stain a fair record."

The red-faced officials demanded to examine the American Indians.

Burke refused. How could he trust them to be impartial? Instead, he told the officials, he and Mr. Salsbury would bring the performers to Washington, D.C., themselves.

The officials grudgingly agreed.

The next morning, the group arrived in the nation's capital. While Salsbury and Burke remained in the hall, the performers filed into a small room at the Interior Department.

Acting Commissioner of Indian Affairs Robert Belt began the questioning. Had any of them been mistreated in any way?

No, they all answered.

"If [the show] did not suit me, I would not remain any longer," noted Rocky Bear.

None of them went hungry either.

"[We] eat everything," Rocky Bear added.

What about the deaths and injuries? prodded Belt. Weren't they due to Cody's neglect?

This time Black Heart spoke. "That is not to be listened to . . . We want to work for these kind of men . . . If Indian wants to work at any place and earn money, he wants to do so; white man got privilege to do same—any kind of work that he wants."

The others agreed. All indicated that they hoped to return to Europe after visiting their families at the Pine Ridge Agency.

Officials were stymied. Ending the investigation, they allowed Burke and Salsbury into the room. Then the annoyed and frustrated Belt dismissed the group. The performers, he said, were free to return to their reservation. At this, the group gave three cheers. Then they hurried out of the room.

A few days later, Bill steamed into New York Harbor. He planned on heading straight for Washington. But as he stepped onto the dock, he was handed a telegram from Major General Nelson Miles.

Come to Chicago immediately, urged the general. He had a mission for the former scout—an important, potentially dangerous, top-secret mission.

Buffalo Bill hopped the first train west.

GHOST DANCE

Bill had returned home at a grim time. Earlier that year, the U.S. government had forced the Sioux to sign an agreement further stripping them of their lands. This time, nine million reservation acres were seized and opened up to settlers. The tracts of cracked, dry earth the American Indians did retain were in the arid region where the average yearly rainfall was less than twenty inches. The Bureau of Indian Affairs' goal of making farmers out of the nomadic Sioux tribes therefore became impossible. No one—neither American Indian nor settler—could grow crops on this land. Despite this, the government cut food rations at Standing Rock and Pine Ridge. This led to starvation and disease.

At this desperate moment, tribes across the Great Plains embraced the new Ghost Dance. Springing from the visions of a Paiute man named Wovoka, the Ghost Dance was a ritual meant to usher in a messiah who would save Native people from the white man's treachery. This messiah "would bring with him all the Indians who had died, and all the departed horses and buffalo. As [the messiah] started east to west, a wave of new earth many feet deep would accompany him, covering the white man and all his works and returning to the living Indian and his departed ancestors the world as it had been before Columbus arrived."

The Ghost Dance was not a call to violence. Its teachings encouraged believers to be moral and honest, to avoid war (with both settlers and other American Indians), and to love one another. Some followers even claimed that Wovoka told them to send their children to school, become farmers, and "help your [Indian] agents." Above all, they were to keep the peace and dance. Dancing, according to one participant, simply allowed them to "make ready to join the ghosts."

By November 1890, the new religion had spread to the Standing Rock Agency. Sitting Bull, too, had shown an interest in the Ghost Dance. As chief, he was obligated to test the new faith. But he never danced, or directed the dances on his reservation. And most historians believe he had doubts about the religion. Still, Indian Agent James McLaughlin saw the Ghost Dance as a chance to be rid of the chief whose influence on the reservation undercut his own. He begged government officials for permission to arrest Sitting Bull.

That's what General Miles wanted to speak with Bill about. Would the showman and former scout undertake a secret mission to arrest his old friend Sitting Bull and bring him to the nearest commanding officer of U.S. troops? The army intended to imprison him at Fort Randall, where he would be separated from his followers.

Bill agreed, although he had no intention of forcing the chief at gunpoint. Instead, he hoped to talk sense and urge peace. He went as Sitting Bull's friend.

Days later, Bill stepped off the train in the rugged frontier town of Bismarck, North Dakota. Still dressed in his businessman's suit and patent-leather shoes, he rented a mule-drawn wagon and filled it with gifts and candy for Sitting Bull. Then he headed south across the snow-covered landscape to Fort Yates and the Standing Rock Agency. "I was sure that if I could reach Sitting Bull he would at least listen to me," said Bill.

He never got the chance. When McLaughlin learned Buffalo Bill was on his way, he frantically telegraphed Washington. Believing he was perfectly capable of dealing with Sitting Bull by himself, he insisted that Bill's orders be rescinded.

When Bill arrived at the Standing Rock Agency, an army messenger handed him a telegram. It was from President Benjamin Harrison, ordering Bill to turn back.

An annoyed Bill obeyed. Driving his still-full wagon to nearby Fort Yates, he caught the first train home to Scout's Rest Ranch.

Two weeks later, McLaughlin attempted to arrest Sitting Bull during an early morning raid on his cabin. The chief's followers resisted. A gun battle broke out.

Hearing the shots, Sitting Bull's horse—the gray pony Bill had given him—thought it was the cue for his Wild West act. As bullets whizzed around him, the riderless pony went through his routine, high-stepping to the left and right, prancing in a circle.

Sitting Bull and eight of his followers fell to the ground, dead.

And the gray pony, coming to the end of his routine, stood in the middle of the carnage and raised one hoof in the air.

Bill was still at the ranch when he heard the news. "Those . . . stupid Indian agents." He spat the words in anger and grief. "Those stupid, panicky, Indian agents."

On December 29, 1890—two weeks after Sitting Bull's death—the Seventh Cavalry arrived near the frozen banks of Wounded Knee Creek, on the Nebraska border. They'd been ordered to escort a band of Lakota men, women, and children who had fled after Sitting Bull's death back to nearby Pine Ridge. When one man balked at handing over his rifle, the nervous soldiers opened fire. The Lakota did their best to fight back. But they were no match for the army's rapid-fire Hotchkiss guns, which hurled exploding shells into the tipis. As men, women, and children fled, troopers chased after them. For hours afterward, the soldiers massacred any American Indians they found, even those who tried to surrender. In one instance, a woman was killed three miles from the site of the main massacre. When the shooting at last ended, between 170 and 190 Native people lay dead. Most were women and children.

Black Elk, who had traveled with the Wild West to England in 1889, but had returned to his people a year later to become a leading Ghost Dancer, raced out to help the survivors. He recalled, "I can still see the butchered women and children lying heaped and scattered all along the crooked gulch . . . And I can see that something else died there in the bloody mud . . . [a] people's dream died there. It was a beautiful dream."

In the following months, soldiers arrested thirty American Indians they believed were the ringleaders of the Ghost Dance outbreak. Now General Miles suggested that Bill take them with him to Europe. This, he reasoned, would remove them from Lakota country, allowing tensions to cool. Even better, the men would see for themselves the

No need to say "the Wild West" is coming. Buffalo Bill is an international star.

advantages of conforming to white civilization. Surely, they would return to their reservations changed men.

Surprisingly, the Bureau of Indian Affairs agreed with Miles. Despite their earlier reluctance to allow Bill to hire Native performers, they now gave permission for the Wild West to take the prisoners.

But did the men want to go?

Twenty-three of them did. When Bill appeared at their prison, Kicking Bear said, "For six weeks I have been a dead man. Now that I see you, I am alive again."

As added incentive, the bureau permitted an additional seventy-five Lakota to also make the journey to Europe. Among them were members of the men's families, an important factor in the prisoners' decision.

Weeks later, Bill and John Burke hustled their new performers onto a ship bound for Europe. Four months earlier they'd returned to the United States fearing that their days of hiring American Indians were over. But now they were returning with more Native performers than ever. A string of tragedies had led, at least for the Wild West, to a startling turn of events.

WILD WEST, HO!

Back at the Wild West's winter camp, Nate Salsbury thought it startling, too. Convinced American Indians would not be allowed to return, he'd begun organizing a gigantic new spectacle. Called the Congress of Rough Riders of the World, it consisted of numerous colorful and exotic horsemen. There were Russian Cossacks, Argentine gauchos, detachments of English and German cavalry, and (later) Syrians and Arabs on desert Thoroughbreds. When Bill and his group arrived the company swelled to an astronomical 650 people!

And so the Wild West—now interwoven with astounding feats of foreign horsemanship—moved across Europe playing to sold-out shows in Germany, Holland, and Britain. Eventually billing itself as Buffalo Bill's Wild West and Congress of Rough Riders of the World, the show struck such a successful formula that the partners would make few changes for the rest of the decade. "The main elements of the Wild West were horses, guns, heroes and villains," noted one historian. "Each act made use of at least one of the elements, and the most complex of them used all four."

In 1893 it returned to the United States for a long and lucrative run in Chicago during the World's Fair. From there it moved on to Brooklyn, New York, for the 1894 season.

In 1895, Nate Salsbury took sick. Unable to manage the big show, the partners formed a business relationship with James Bailey, former partner of P. T. Barnum (who had died four years earlier) and owner of the largest circus in the country. Under Bailey's management, the Wild West took to the rails, traveling over 9,000 miles in 190 days to 131 cities. It continued this grueling schedule for the next four seasons. By 1899, under pressure from Bailey, the Wild West added a circus sideshow. For an additional charge, visitors could gawp at a snake charmer, a Japanese magician, a sword swallower, and glassblowers from Venice. In that last season of the nineteenth century, the show traveled 11,110 miles.

Buffalo Bill bows a farewell salute to his audience (1913).

ACT EIGHT

SHOW'S END
OR
"SALUTE."

—Buffalo Bill's Wild West Program, 1894

A SCENE FROM THE WILD WEST

The dust settles. The sound of gunfire fades. Could it truly be over? Two hours have passed so quickly! Showgoers are left spellbound, breathless, exhilarated.

In the arena, the whole company assembles once more—the Lakota still in paint and feathers; the vaqueros and cowboys; the black-bearded Cossacks and the Arabs in white headdresses; the chasseurs and cuirassiers from the armies of Germany, France, and England; detachments from the U.S. cavalry; South American gauchos; frontiersmen, rough riders, Texas rangers. With dash and spirit they charge once more around the arena before disappearing behind the white canvas curtain.

Only Buffalo Bill remains. On his white horse, he rides forward. His gaze lingers on his audience for a moment. Then sweeping off his sombrero, he flourishes it in a final salute.

Many in the audience raise their hands in reply. They wave goodbye to their hero. They bid farewell to their friend.

Still holding his pose, he nods in heartfelt acknowledgment. Then he reins his horse backward until he, too, disappears behind the parted curtains.

Buffalo Bill is gone.

The show is over.

The Cowboy Band strikes up a tune and the audience departs for their farms or for small towns or big cities. They take with them popcorn balls and programs and memories. Memories of a vanishing frontier. Memories reshaped into myth and retold by Bill Cody. Memories based on his life.

Many believe they saw the real West that day.

LIFE WITHOUT BILL

While Bill traveled the world, back in North Platte his family made do without him.

He wasn't there in November 1889 to walk Arta down the aisle when she married Horton Boal in the most lavish wedding the town had ever seen. He did, however, send his congratulations and a check for five thousand dollars.

He wasn't there in November 1890 to pace the parlor floor when Arta gave birth to his first grandchild, Arta Clara Boal. He got a second chance to pace in March 1896 when his namesake, William Cody Boal, was born. But show business kept him away that time, too.

As for little Irma, Bill missed watching his rough-and-tumble daughter grow up. Scrappy like her father, Irma was "wilder than a goldurned coyote," recalled one playmate. She got into fistfights with boys and let slip the occasional curse word. But Bill rarely got to admire her gumption. In hopes of polishing off those rough edges, Lulu sent Irma to Miss Brown's Boarding School in New York City. After that, the girl saw little of North Platte and even less of her father.

Despite the angelic expression captured in this 1897 photograph, Irma Cody (then thirteen) was a fearless, impulsive, troublemaking tomboy. While her mother tried desperately to squelch Irma's unladylike behaviors, her father encouraged them.

He missed Irma's wedding, too, in February 1903, although he did send a cablegram wishing the couple "all joy and happiness."

And he wasn't there to wave from the dock when she and her new husband sailed for the Philippine Islands just weeks later. He wouldn't see her again for two long years.

Bill regretted it. No matter where he traveled, and despite his problems with Lulu, he pined for North Platte. He longed to sit on the velvety lawn of his ranch and smoke a cigar with his friends. He wanted to take long carriage rides with his daughters. And he was forever thinking up ways to improve Scout's Rest. He dreamed of another barn: "I thought I would paint this [one] white," he wrote to Al Goodman from Europe. "Then in the spring we could put a fresh coat of red paint on the Big Barn, and paint the House blue . . . I want to try a hundred acres of alfalfa. Do you know a good farmer I can hire by the year?"

So why didn't Bill simply retire from show business?

He couldn't afford it. Despite making huge sums of money in these years, he was in a perpetual financial bind. This came from his continued money-losing schemes—a printing press, a newspaper. "I have lost several fortunes in outside ventures," he told reporters in 1900.

He was about to lose several more.

A TOWN CALLED CODY

It didn't look like Buffalo Bill's advertisements. Where were the "perfect homes" and the "verdant mountain valley"? Nora Haight's heart sank. Was *this* what she'd traveled all the way from New York for? Cody, Wyoming, was nothing but a sandy sagebrush flat located high above the Shoshone River. Yes, the river looked pretty, fringed as it was with cottonwoods and grassy bottoms. But its smell probably caused Nora to wrinkle her nose. Its sulfurous water reeked. No wonder it earned the nickname "stinking water."

As for the town itself, there was hardly a tree in sight. But there were plenty of saloons, ten in all. They were squeezed onto one block, along with two general stores that carried everything from groceries to house paint, two butcher shops selling meat tough as shoe leather, two banks, a drugstore, and a cigar shop. Nora noted that the tailor shop was located smack dab in the middle of the saloons. "I have to brave it if I go in there," she told herself. "One never knows when some man will be suddenly thrown out on the street from one."

One never knew when Buffalo Bill would make an appearance either. Since 1895, he'd been trying to make a go of the town. He and his partners had sunk a fortune into irrigation canals in hopes of turning the desert into farmable land. When the canals hadn't paid, Bill turned his attention to other schemes—selling lots, buying interest in a coal company, and opening the Buffalo Bill Barn with coaches and rigs for hire. He even built a grand hotel. Named the Irma after his youngest daughter, it had fine furnishings, a grand piano in the parlor, and a sixteen-foot wraparound porch. It also boasted an enormous cherrywood bar. Made in France, the bar had been shipped first to the east coast, then by train to Montana, and finally by wagon to Cody. It was rumored to have cost Buffalo Bill a whopping $100,000 ($2.7 million in today's money).

His sister Julia, widowed in 1901, had come out to run the hotel with her two youngest children. She worked hard to make it a paying establishment despite her brother's impractical dreams. He had big plans to expand. Time and again, Julia told him there was no need. There simply wasn't enough business. For all his efforts, only two hundred people, including Nora Haight, had moved to Cody. And tourists weren't exactly pouring in.

But Bill was convinced Cody would make him a fortune, enough to retire from show business. More important, he would be leaving a real mark on the country as the founder of a town. "I want to be known as a pioneer and developer of civilization rather than a scout and

Bill, mounted on Isham, poses before the Irma Hotel in Cody, Wyoming (c. 1913). Standing immediately to the left is Lulu.

showman," he confessed. And so he kept dumping money into the enterprise.

He put himself into it, too. After 1901, he began spending the show's off-season at his new ranch, the T E, located thirty-five miles southwest of the town. Now he spent the snow-deep winters there—far from Lulu—in a small white house he'd had built. Many times he braved the subzero temperatures to visit new settlers. "He always had words of encouragement and complimented them on the splendid home they had started and improvements they had made," recalled one resident. Other times he rode into town. Dropping into stores and saloons, he asked folks, "How [are you] getting along? . . . What kind of farming [are you] doing?"

Even while he was traveling with the Wild West, his mind was never far from Cody. He hatched a plan to locate a military academy for boys near the town and tried to establish a retirement home for the Elks lodge in Cody. He began working on plans to connect the town with Yellowstone National Park via a stagecoach line, then began building a string of hotels along the line to accommodate the tourists he was sure would be coming. And he racked his brains trying to work out a way to develop a nearby hot springs. All this would, he believed, do much to bring settlers into the area.

A 1911 photo of Bill's T E Ranch, his home outside Cody, Wyoming.

Still, the town grew slowly. "That dear old country eats up my money faster than I can make it," admitted Bill. No, he wasn't making a fortune. But he had found a new home.

CODY V. CODY

The idea of divorcing Lulu once again swirled in Bill's mind. Why should he remain married to a woman he hadn't seen or spoken to in years? "God did not intend joining two people for [them] to go through life miserable," he reasoned. Besides, he'd been generous to Lulu. He'd given her not only all the North Platte property (except for Scout's Rest Ranch) but an annual income, too. All he wanted in return was a quick and quiet separation. Would she do it?

Absolutely not, replied Lulu. She wasn't walking away without a fight.

"Then it's war and publicity," declared Bill. He filed for divorce in January 1904.

The news caused a scandal. Not only was divorce frowned on by society in those days, but Buffalo Bill's image was that of a family man. Show programs included pictures of his cozy home in North Platte and sappy poems written to his daughters. So audiences were shocked by their hero's desire to tear apart his own family after thirty-eight years of marriage. "We're Liable to Hear Some Naughty Things," declared a headline in the *North Platte Telegraph*.

Bad publicity or not, Bill was going through with it. "I think I am entitled to be at peace in my old age," he told Julia. "And I surely can't have it with Lulu."

A month later, the couple's thirty-seven-year-old daughter, Arta, died. Doctors claimed she'd died due to complications from surgery.

But Lulu insisted she'd died of a broken heart caused by her father's behavior. Bill Cody had killed his own child, she declared. And she wanted him charged with murder.

Friends managed to calm her down long enough for the funeral. Together, the estranged couple accompanied Arta's body to the cemetery in Rochester where two of their children already rested. For most of the journey, they did not speak to each other. And they refused to ride in the same carriage from the train station to the burial site.

But Lulu's grief and anger could not be contained. On the way back, while changing trains in Chicago, she erupted. "It's your fault!" she screamed at Bill's sister May as onlookers gaped. "I will bring you Codys so low the dogs won't bark at you."

She was as good as her word. In a drawn-out courtroom battle, the public learned about Bill's long absences from home, his heavy drinking, and his affairs with other women.

"Do you still love Mr. Cody?" one lawyer asked Lulu.

Her answer had the ring of truth when she replied, "Yes I do. I would gladly welcome him home."

Both the court and the newspaper-reading public dismissed Bill's reasons for divorce, among them extreme cruelty and financial sabotage. They took Lulu's side. The judge refused to grant a divorce. The Codys, he ruled, would stay married.

But that didn't mean they had to see each other ever again.

SAYING GOODBYE AGAIN
AND AGAIN AND AGAIN

The fortune-teller who'd read Mary Cody's palm so many years earlier had been right. Her son's name had become known the world over. Seventeen hundred dime novels featuring Buffalo Bill Cody had been published; tens of thousands of posters showing him on a white horse had been circulated. Millions of people on both sides of the Atlantic had seen him perform—presidents, royalty, celebrities. Children everywhere looked up to him. Women longed to kiss his cheek. Men wanted to shake his hand.

But fame could not keep his creditors away. He was always racing to stay ahead of his bills. Cody, Wyoming, had not panned out. But by 1903, he believed he'd finally found a surefire way to a fortune: a gold mine in Arizona. "Say, isn't it glorious to think your old brother [will be] a millionaire?" he wrote Julia optimistically.

Eagerly, he dropped almost all his earnings into the mine. When that wasn't enough, he sold off Scout's Rest Ranch and the Irma Hotel and sank that cash into the mine, too. He wholeheartedly believed that at any moment he would strike it rich and his retirement would be secure. "I'll stick right to my work of rustling up money to keep things going while you are at work on that end," he wrote to the mine's manager.

Johnny Baker wasn't as convinced. Over the years, Bill's faithful foster son had taken on more and more of the show's responsibilities—purchasing livestock, counting ticket sales, and supervising the arena during performances. Suspicious about Bill's latest investment, Johnny paid the mine a surprise visit. He found just four men working, although the payroll listed thirty-six names. When he returned to the show, he told Bill the mine wasn't properly managed. He advised the showman to be more cautious.

Skeptics, sometimes even including his own partners, gave Bill little credit for handling the Wild West's business details. But this photo taken around 1905 shows Cody hard at work in his tent, planning the show's railroad route.

Bill didn't listen. Believing the million-dollar payload was just out of reach, he built wagon roads and railroad tracks, and installed a water system. It cost a fortune.

In 1908, in hopes of wringing more money from the Wild West, he formed a new partnership with Gordon William "Pawnee Bill" Lillie. (Nate Salsbury had died in 1902; James Bailey followed in 1906.) The merger was successful, especially when they concocted the idea of a two-year "Farewell Tour." Since Bill planned on retiring soon, the partners figured it was good business to stop at every city he'd ever played. Audiences would come out in droves to see the old scout one last time. And they would make buckets of money.

They did. Crowds packed the arenas. And at the end of each performance, a white-haired Buffalo Bill, now sixty-four years old, rode forward to address the audience: "When I went away from here each year before I merely said good-night," he said at the end of each speech. "This time it will mean good-bye. To my little friends in the gallery and the grown-ups who used to sit there, I thank you once again. God bless you all—good-bye." Then, with a final wave of his sombrero, he backed slowly away on his white stallion Isham. Rising to its feet, the audience cheered. "There was not a dry eye in the [house]," recalled one show worker.

Profits from the Farewell Tour were immense. Lillie used his share to build a new house on his Oklahoma ranch. Bill dumped his into the mine. Meanwhile, his debts piled up. He owed money everywhere. Realizing he couldn't afford to retire from show business, he extended his farewell tour. "Just one more good season," he kept saying.

A COUPLE ONCE MORE

Five years. That's how long the Codys had gone without seeing each other. And yet, on this steamy July day in 1910, Bill found himself

Together again—Bill and Lulu in 1916, six years after their reconciliation.

pacing in the parlor of his wife's North Platte house. Why was he there? Because of his only living child, Irma.

Despite all that had happened between them, Irma believed her parents' marriage could be salvaged. Over the years, she had talked calmly with her mother. She had argued sensibly with her father. Neither was getting any younger, she pointed out. Wouldn't it be a comfort to spend their final years together?

Perhaps it was financial strain or exhaustion. But Bill came around to the idea first. The man who'd publicly sued for divorce now sent his wife a letter asking to be "forgiven for the past." Lulu replied that she was "willing, but some things must be understood between them." What things? No one knows for sure. But Bill obviously accepted her conditions.

Shortly after, she joined her husband on tour and Bill was writing, "We've had peaceful and loving trips together . . . We've traveled to Arizona . . . and she loves to read or knit on the veranda of the inn while I look after our mining interests. She's less of a homebody now."

The couple even threw a party to celebrate their forty-fifth wedding anniversary in 1911. "I have forgotten all our tribulations," Bill said in his toast, "and remember only the good in our union."

Then Bill returned to the road. And Lulu packed up her North Platte house and moved to Cody, Wyoming.

BUSTED!

On July 21, 1913, just minutes after the Denver performance ended, Bill saw the sheriff and his men fan out across the lot. He knew what it meant. Creditors had foreclosed on the show. Its assets were being seized.

Bill signaled to one of the workers. Quick, he instructed, hurry over to the ticket window and save the day's profits. Without it, he knew, he would not be able to pay his performers or even buy food for them or the animals.

The worker rushed for the wagon. But the sheriff got there first and took the cash box, along with everything else in sight—tents, seats, even the company's trunks. The show people were left penniless, with only the shirts on their backs. The show animals were left without food and shelter.

While Lillie hurried off to New Jersey for legal advice, Bill devoted himself to helping the stranded workers. Scraping together what little cash he could, he divided it among them. And when a friend wired five hundred dollars, he split that, too. Using all his charm and influence, he found an inexpensive stable for the dozens of horses.

Soon the show people moved in with them, sleeping in the hay and washing their clothes out in the troughs so they could wear them the next day. This hand-to-mouth existence lasted for weeks. Stranded, many troupers took jobs where they could. Not until it was clear that all the show's belongings would be auctioned off to pay Bill's debts did they finally give up. Some remained in the area. Others set off for home on foot. A few of the American Indians even sold their show costumes to get back to their reservations.

Determined to make things up to his loyal troupers, Bill began making plans to start over. No matter that he was sixty-seven years old and up to his neck in debt. "I am not down and out," he told a friend. "I will soon be on the road with a new and better show."

But all his optimism could not keep his show from being sold out from under him.

THE STORY OF ISHAM

The day of the sale, a downhearted Bill wandered along a Denver sidewalk.

That's when he bumped into Colonel Bills, an old friend from Nebraska. "Are you going to the sale?" the colonel asked.

"I don't care to go," replied Bill. His eyes filled with tears. "I can stand to see everything else in the show sold, but I can't bear to see Isham, the faithful horse who has carried me for over twenty years, sold to strangers."

The colonel didn't press. He went off to the sale, and Bill walked on.

Hours later, the two met again.

"Has Isham been sold?" asked Bill.

Yes, replied the colonel.

Bill wanted to know the new owner's name. "I hope he will treat the old horse kindly," he said.

221

"I am sure Isham will be treated with kindness," replied the colonel. He paused, then added, "By none other than his master of twenty years."

It took a moment for Bill to grasp the truth. The colonel had bought Isham for him!

Recalled the colonel, "[Bill] broke down and tears fell from his cheeks. His simple words of thanks were worth more to me than the trouble it took to buy the horse for his old master."

END OF THE TRAIL

To pay his debts, Bill went to work for the Sells-Floto Circus, a second-rate traveling show with mildewed show tents and rotten ropes. His contract didn't require him to perform any reenactments or shooting acts. All he had to do was ride out and introduce the show from the saddle. But it was humiliating work. The show was not his own, and Bill had to put up with the circus's unscrupulous owner, Henry Tammen. "I am very tired and nervous and discouraged," he wrote Julia. "Everything I attempt to do goes wrong."

He still had hopes for the gold mine, but they were fading fast. To raise money, he rented some of his land in Wyoming and began writing a series of autobiographical articles called "The Great West That Was: Buffalo Bill's Life Story" for *Hearst International Magazine*. But he still did not have nearly enough to pay what he owed. The worn-out showman kept performing.

In 1916 he left Sells-Floto and took a job with another traveling show, the Miller Brothers and Arlington 101 Ranch Wild West. For a hundred dollars a day, he led the parade and introduced the show from the saddle.

He would have preferred riding around the arena in a carriage. At seventy, his once strong body was exhausted. Gaunt and pale, he suffered from constant pain due to kidney problems that made sitting a horse agony. But audiences hadn't paid to see Buffalo Bill wave from a fancy rig. And so day in and day out he climbed into the saddle. Faithful Johnny Baker, whose face now bore a few wrinkles where his boyish freckles had once been, was with him. Johnny had to hoist the old scout up onto his horse at showtime. Slumped in the saddle, eyes closed and grimacing from the pain, Bill waited for his cue. Then the curtain opened. Straightening his shoulders, he spurred his horse into the spotlight. He kept his chin high and his hat waving as he galloped around the arena. The audience applauded wildly. Look, they cried, it's Buffalo Bill!

Minutes later, back in the shadows, Bill slumped again, barely able to hold on. Gently, Johnny eased the man he called his foster father out of the saddle and back to his private train car.

THE LAST RIDE

Bill's train pulled into Glenwood Springs, Colorado, on January 3, 1917. For the last few months, since the close of the show's season, he'd been feeling poorly. First he'd gotten a terrible cold, followed by a mysterious stomach ailment. Then he'd begun suffering from chest pains. Heart trouble, his doctor had diagnosed. He'd suggested Bill take the mineral waters at the springs.

At the depot, reporters clustered around him. Were the rumors true? they asked. Was he seriously ill? Close to dying?

Bill laughed them off. "I've still got my boots on," he replied, and claimed that after a few days of restorative waters, he'd be fit as a fiddle.

Forty-eight hours later he collapsed from what some described as a nervous breakdown. He couldn't remember anything that had happened over the past few days. His mind wandered. Doctors transferred him to his sister May's house in nearby Denver. Delirious, he kept telling those around him, "Soon [I] will go on the road with a new show, bigger and better than ever."

Lulu and Irma raced from Cody to be by his side. So did Julia. The change in his appearance shocked them. He was, recalled Lulu, "frail, white-faced . . . long white hair clinging about his temples, the lips thin and white and wan."

Still, he fought. Patting Lulu's tearstained cheek, he said, "The doctor says I'm going to die, does he? Well, I'm pretty much alive right now, ain't I? I'll be alright."

The world, however, knew the truth. Telegraph wires across the country carried the news: Buffalo Bill was dying in Denver. Newspapermen kept vigil on his sister May's front porch, reporting hourly on his health. Some claimed the old scout played cards during his last hours. Recalled his grandson, William Cody Boal, "We played a game of high five . . . His opponents sluffed a trick on him, and even in his weakened condition he called them on it. He was always a square shooter and demanded fair play."

Others claimed his mind trailed back to his touring days. "He would imagine that he was on the road," his nephew William Cody Bradford recalled. "He would ask me where we were and what time it was when we got in . . . In fact, he lived his life over. He done just as he did when he was on the road with the show."

Old friends visited to pay their respects. To them, Bill appeared serene and accepting. "The old scout was in pajamas and slippers, and over them was drawn a housecoat," remembered one. "Just the man himself, standing there, waxen pale . . . his hand out in a last farewell . . . It was the last time. I knew it; he knew it; we all knew it. But on the surface not a sign."

Bill's biggest concern was that Johnny Baker get there in time. "I wish Johnny would come," he said again and again.

A passerby snapped this final picture of Bill in Glenwood Springs, Colorado, on January 6, 1917, as the old scout stood outside the stone bathhouse where he'd gone to take the medicinal waters. Four days later, he died.

But Johnny, who was racing across the country on the night train from New York, would arrive too late to say goodbye. On January 10, 1917, at a few minutes past noon, Bill Cody died. Instantly the news flashed around the world: "the greatest plainsman the world ever knew" was dead.

His body, taken from his sister's house, lay in state for three days beneath the golden dome of the Colorado State Capitol rotunda. Twenty-five thousand people lined up to pay their respects. Tributes flooded in from the king of England, President Woodrow Wilson, generals, old colleagues, and ordinary folks who'd seen him perform in his Wild West. Among the messages was this note from the Pine Ridge Agency:

> The Oglala Sioux Indians of Pine Ridge, South Dakota, in council assembled, resolve that expression of deepest sympathy be extended . . . on behalf of all the Oglalas to the wife, relatives and friends of the late William F. Cody (Buffalo Bill) for the loss they have suffered; that these people . . . may know that the Oglalas found in Buffalo Bill a warm and lasting friend; that our hearts are sad from the heavy burden of his passing, lightening only in the belief of our meeting before . . . our Wakan Takan in the great hunting ground.

The following June, the weather finally permitting, Bill was laid to rest atop Lookout Mountain, twenty miles from Denver. Some people said he'd wanted to be buried in the hills near Cody, but Lulu claimed he'd changed his mind at the end. "It's pretty up there [on Lookout Mountain]," he'd told her. "You can look down into four states."

Colorado. Nebraska. Wyoming. Utah. Four western, though no

longer wild, states. The frontier was gone. But myth remained. Forged in part by boyhood memories and a Wild West show seen by millions of people, the myth was full of blazing guns, galloping horses, and vanquished warriors. And at its center rode a buckskin-clad hero on a big white horse. "Let my show go on," Bill reportedly whispered on his deathbed.

As long as the myth continues, it will.

Created for the 1890 European tour, Bill's image is made up of guns, ropes, snowshoes, and—weirdly—buffalo and horse heads.

AFTERWORD

Writing this book has been both a joy and a frustration—a joy because I learned about the indefatigable Will Cody, a frustration because what I read wasn't always true. The man didn't always tell the truth. What were his real achievements? What were his fabrications? It was hard to tell. Will, as I discovered, often mixed his real achievements with colorful fiction as a way of mythologizing his own life. He reshaped his experiences to fit the frontier stories he told his audiences. And he left me with no choice but to question *all* of his claims.

Take, for instance, his autobiography. Written in 1879, when he was still performing onstage in theaters, it was meant to enhance his frontiersman reputation and star qualities. Despite the book's many exaggerations, it is full of what historians believe to be Will's own phrasings and tone. It contains plenty of firsthand knowledge about personalities and events. As such, it stands as the most trustworthy version of his life from childhood to age thirty.

In later years, however, his press agents churned out revised editions of the autobiography. Much of what they added was pure hokum. Suddenly, they had him trailing gangs of desperate outlaws, spying for the army, and rescuing Indian maidens in distress. Not a lick of it was true. It was all taken directly from the pages of popular dime novels. Still, these tall tales were repeated again and again as truth. Before long, they were embedded in his life story.

To chisel out the truth, I turned to other primary sources. At the McCracken Research Library at the Buffalo Bill Center of the West in Cody, Wyoming, I looked through hundreds of photographs and searched out reams of original newspaper articles. I pored over microfilm copies of Cody's scrapbooks, sifted through pages of private letters, and read stacks of original pamphlets, programs, and travel logs.

I also read memoirs written by family, friends, and associates. I took these with a grain of salt, too. While some accounts, like Julia Cody Goodman's memoir, offered a corrective to her brother's tales, others merely agreed with his highly publicized recollections. Once again, I was forced to match their words against the historical record.

Next, I turned to historians. What did they have to say about his life and lies? There are hundreds of books about William F. Cody. Dozens of scholars have made the study of the American West their life's work. They've written insightful, enlightening books and articles that have shaped my own thoughts on the subject. Without their work, I could never have completed the excavation process that led to this book. I might not have even known where to start digging.

I am especially indebted to Dr. Jeffrey Means (enrolled member of the Oglala Sioux Tribe), associate professor of history at the University of Wyoming in the field of Native American history, for bringing his vast expertise in Great Plains Indian culture and colonial cultural encounters in the eighteenth and nineteenth centuries to this manuscript by reading portions of it and offering valuable criticism.

I am also grateful to Dr. Louis S. Warren, W. Turrentine Jackson Professor of Western U.S. History at the University of California, Davis, and author of *Buffalo Bill's America: William Cody and the Wild West Show*, for pointing me in the direction of the latest Cody scholarship and meticulously fact-checking the completed manuscript.

This book owes much to both men's boundless knowledge.

BIBLIOGRAPHY

ARCHIVAL MATERIAL DEPOSITORIES

BBCW: Buffalo Bill Center of the West's Harold McCracken Research Library, William F. Cody (Buffalo Bill) Collection, Cody, Wyoming.

DPL: Denver Public Library's Western History Department, William F. Cody Collection, Denver, Colorado.

NARA: National Archives and Records Administration, Washington, D.C.

WSA: Wyoming State Archives, William F. Cody's testimony in *Cody v. Cody*, Civil Case File 970, Folder 2, Cheyenne, Wyoming.

BOOKS AND MAGAZINES

PRIMARY SOURCE MATERIALS

Black Elk and John Neihardt. *Black Elk Speaks: Being the Life Story of a Holy Man of the Oglala Sioux.* Albany: State University of New York Press, 2008.

Blackstone, Sarah J. *The Business of Being Buffalo Bill: Selected Letters of William F. Cody, 1879–1917.* New York: Praeger, 1988.

Boal, Maj. William Cody. *My Grandfather . . . "Buffalo Bill."* North Platte, NE: privately published, 1956.

Bratt, John. *Trails of Yesteryear.* Chicago: University Publishing Company, 1921.

Burke, John. *Buffalo Bill from Prairie to Palace.* Chicago: Rand McNally, 1893.

Cody, Louisa F., and Courtney Ryley Cooper. *Memories of Buffalo Bill by His Wife.* New York: D. Appleton and Company, 1919.

Cody, William F. *An Autobiography of Buffalo Bill.* New York: Cosmopolitan Book Corporation, 1920.

———. *Buffalo Bill's Life Story.* New York: Skyhorse Publishing, 2010 (reprint of Time-Life Books 1982 reprint of first edition, published in 1879 by F. E. Bliss).

———. "Famous Hunting Parties of the Plains." *Cosmopolitan* 17, no. 2 (June 1894): 137–40.

———. *Life and Adventures of Buffalo Bill.* Chicago: Stanton and Van Vliet Company, 1917.

————. *Story of the Wild West and Camp Fire Chats by Buffalo Bill (Hon. W. F. Cody): A Full and Complete History of the Renowned Pioneer Quartet, Boone, Crockett, Carson and Buffalo Bill.* Philadelphia: Historical Publishing Company, 1888.

————. *True Tales of the Plains.* New York: Empire Book Company, 1908.

Davies, Hugh. *Ten Days on the Plains.* New York: Crocker & Company, 1871.

Fellows, Dexter, and Andrew A. Freeman. *This Way to the Big Show: The Life of Dexter Fellows.* New York: Viking, 1936.

Foote, Stella. *Letters from "Buffalo Bill."* Billings, MT: Foote, 1954.

Fulton, Frances I. Sims. *To and Through Nebraska by a Pennsylvania Girl.* Lincoln, NE: Journal Company State Printers, 1884.

Goodman, Julia Cody. "Julia Cody Goodman's Memoirs of Buffalo Bill." Edited by Don Russell. *Kansas Historical Quarterly* 28, no. 4 (Winter 1962): 442–96.

Hafen, Leroy R., and Ann W., eds. *Mormon Resistance: A Documentary Account of the Utah Expedition, 1857–58.* Glendale, CA: A. H. Clark, 1958.

Hawkeye, Harry. *Buffalo Bill, King of the Scouts: A Narrative of Thrilling Adventures and Graphic Description of Frontier Life.* Chicago: J. Regan & Company, 1908.

Klumpke, Anna. *Rosa Bonheur: The Artist's (Auto)biography.* Translated by Gretchen van Slyke. Ann Arbor: University of Michigan Press, 1997.

Leonard, Elizabeth, and Julia Cody Goodman. *Buffalo Bill: King of the Old West.* New York: Library Publishers, 1955.

Lindsey, David, ed. "The Journal of an 1859 Pike's Peak Gold Seeker," *Kansas Historical Quarterly* 22, no. 4 (Winter 1856): 305–20.

Lovejoy, Julia Louisa. "Letters from Kanzas [*sic*]," *Kansas Historical Quarterly* 11, no. 1 (February 1942): 29–44.

Majors, Alexander. *Seventy Years on the Frontier.* Chicago: Rand McNally, 1893.

McLaughlin, James. *My Friend the Indian.* Lincoln: University of Nebraska Press, 1899.

Millbrook, Minnie Drubbs. "Big Game Hunting with the Custers, 1869–1870." *Kansas Historical Quarterly* 41, no. 4 (Winter 1975): 429–34.

Paul, R. Eli, ed. *The Nebraska-Indian Wars Reader, 1865–1877.* Lincoln: University of Nebraska Press, 1998.

Pierson, Michael D. "A War of Extermination: A Newly Uncovered Letter of Julia Louisa Lovejoy, 1856." *Kansas History* 16 (Summer 1993): 120–22.

Pratt, Richard Henry. *Battlefield and Classroom: Four Decades with the American Indian, 1867–1904.* Norman: University of Oklahoma Press, 1964.

Putnam, John H. "A Trip to the End of the Union Pacific in 1868." *Kansas Historical Quarterly* 13, no. 3 (August 1944): 196–203.

Salsbury, Nate. "The Origins of the Wild West Show." *Colorado Magazine* 32, no. 3 (July 1955): 200–15.

Samuels, Peggy, and Harold Samuels, eds. *The Collected Writings of Frederic Remington.* Garden City, NY: Doubleday, 1979.

Sheridan, General Philip H. *Personal Memoirs.* 2 volumes. New York: Charles L. Webster & Company, 1888.

Thomas, Chauncey. "Buffalo Bill's Last Interview." *Outdoor Life* 34, no. 5 (May 1917): 487–99.

Wetmore, Helen Cody. *Last of the Great Scouts.* New York: Grosset & Dunlap, 1918.

Yellow Robe, Chauncey. "The Menace of the Wild West Show." *Quarterly Journal of American Indians* 2, no. 1 (January–March 1914): 225.

SECONDARY SOURCE MATERIALS

Blackstone, Sarah J. *Buckskin, Bullets and Business: A History of Buffalo Bill's Wild West.* Westport, CT: Greenwood Press, 1986.

Botkin, B. A., ed. *A Treasury of American Folklore.* New York: Crown, 1944.

Castel, Albert. *A Frontier State at War: Kansas, 1861–1865.* Ithaca, NY: Cornell University Press, 1958.

Corbett, Christopher. *Orphans Preferred: The Twisted Truth and Lasting Legend of the Pony Express.* New York: Broadway Books, 2004.

Enss, Chris. *Buffalo Gals: Women of Buffalo Bill's Wild West Show.* Guilford, CT: Twodot, 2006.

———. *The Many Loves of Buffalo Bill: The True Story of Life on the Wild West Show.* Guilford, CT: Twodot, 2010.

Eyal, Yonatan. "With His Eyes Open: Stephen A. Douglas and the Kansas-Nebraska Disaster of 1854." *Journal of the Illinois State Historical Society* 91, no. 4 (Winter 1998): 175–217.

Goodrich, Thomas. *Black Flag: Guerilla Warfare on the Western Border, 1861–1865.* Bloomington: Indiana University Press, 1999.

Gray, John S. "Fact Versus Fiction in the Kansas Boyhood of Buffalo Bill." *Kansas History* 8 (Spring 1985): 2–20.

Kasson, Joy. *Buffalo Bill's Wild West: Celebrity, Memory and Popular History*. New York: Hill and Wang, 2000.

Leonard, L. O. "Buffalo Bill's First Wild West Rehearsal." *Union Pacific Magazine* (August 1922): 22–29.

Lockwood, Frank C. *The Life of Edward C. Ayer*. Chicago: A. C. McClurg and Company, 1929.

Logan, Herschel C. *Buckskin and Satin: The Life of Texas Jack J. B. Omohundro*. Harrisburg, PA: Stackpole Company, 1954.

McMaster, John Bach. *A History of the People of the United States, from the Revolution to the Civil War*. Vol 8. 1850–1861. New York: D. Appleton and Company, 1921.

McMurtry, Larry. *The Colonel and Little Missie*. New York: Simon & Schuster Paperbacks, 2005.

McNenly, Linda Scarangella. *Native Performers in Wild West Shows from Buffalo Bill to Euro Disney*. Norman: University of Oklahoma Press, 2012.

Monaghan, Jay. *The Great Rascal: The Life and Adventures of Ned Buntline*. Boston: Little, Brown, 1951.

Moses, L. G. *Wild West Shows and the Images of American Indians, 1883–1933*. Albuquerque: University of New Mexico Press, 1996.

Nichols, Alice. *Bleeding Kansas*. New York: Oxford University Press, 1954.

Pfaller, Louis. "'Enemies in '76, Friends in '85': Sitting Bull and Buffalo Bill." *Prologue: The Journal of the National Archives* 1 (Fall 1969): 16–31.

Rosa, Joseph G., and Robin May. *Buffalo Bill and His Wild West: A Pictorial Biography*. Lawrence: University Press of Kansas, 1989.

Russell, Don. *The Lives and Legends of Buffalo Bill*. Norman: University of Oklahoma Press, 1960.

Sayers, Isabelle S. *Annie Oakley and Buffalo Bill's Wild West*. New York: Dover, 1981.

Sell, Henry Blackman, and Victoria Weybright. *Buffalo Bill and the Wild West*. New York: Oxford University Press, 1955.

Utley, Robert M. *Sitting Bull: The Life and Times of an American Patriot*. New York: Holt Paperbacks, 1993.

Vestal, Stanley. *Sitting Bull, Champion of the Sioux: A Biography*. Norman: University of Oklahoma Press, 1957.

Walsh, Richard J., and Milton Salsbury. *The Making of Buffalo Bill: A Study in Heroics*. Indianapolis: Bobbs-Merrill, 1928.

Warren, Louis S. *Buffalo Bill's America: William Cody and the Wild West Show*. New York: Alfred A. Knopf, 2005.

Yost, Nellie Snyder. *Buffalo Bill: His Family, Friends, Fame, Failures and Fortunes*. Chicago: Sage Books, 1979.

SCOUTING FOR BUFFALO BILL ONLINE

To discover more about Buffalo Bill and his world, try these sites:

Buffalo Bill Museum and Grave

With over thirteen hundred archival photographs ranging from family portraits to behind-the-scene peeks at the Wild West, this website is a visual treat for those wanting to see even more.

buffalobill.org

Buffalo Bill Center of the West

Browse through a portion of the incredible collection of Cody artifacts and documents housed at this museum and research library. A virtual tour of sorts, this website allows viewers to see photos of Bill's buckskin coat, read his personal letters, and peruse scrapbooks and travel logs. Links are provided to other museums with related materials, such as the Cody Firearms Museum and the Plains Indian Museum, also part of the BBCW.

centerofthewest.org

William F. Cody Archive

A joint project of the University of Nebraska–Lincoln and the McCracken Research Library at the BBCW, the William F. Cody Archive is a vast repository of online books, letters, articles, photographs, and much more. Especially fascinating are the associated works of statesmen, military leaders, and royalty, all of which enlarge viewers' understanding of the growth and expansion of the American West.

codyarchive.org

And these websites are just for fun:

Listen to a reenactment of the music played more than a century ago during Wild West performances

centerofthewest.org/explore/buffalo-bill/research/buffalo-bill-band

Hear Buffalo Bill speak

youtube.com/watch?v=1U-N1dVt8RA

Marvel at Annie Oakley's sharpshooting abilities

youtube.com/watch?v=dQSTSNq5dOM

Watch Buffalo Bill and Chief Iron Tail swap stories in sign language, and see the bronco busters and other Buffalo Bill videos

codyarchive.org/category/result.html?q=subCategory%3A%22Video%22

And take a front-row seat during the Wild West's 1909 and 1910 seasons. See Johnny Baker shoot glass balls from the sky, experience the "Attack on the Deadwood Stage" and the "Battle of Summit Springs," and get a glimpse of Buffalo Bill performing his famous re-creation of a buffalo hunt.

youtube.com/watch?v=g3meHAqxuDI

Need more? Try this glimpse of bronco busting and American Indian dancing. Be sure to watch for Buffalo Bill's "Salute" at the end.

youtube.com/watch?v=kjIH5AUglos

SOURCE NOTES

For those materials found in archival depositories, I chose not to include box numbers in the citations. Over time, collections can be moved into different containers, but because the original order of the documents never changes, the information included in the citations will provide the exact location of the document regardless of the box number.

FANFARE

4   "There's nothing fake": "Opening of the American Exhibition Buffalo Bill's Wild West," *Lloyd's Weekly Newspaper*, n.d. in Annie Oakley Scrapbook, 1887, BBCW.

5   "Welcome, your Majesty": Wetmore, p. 266.

ACT ONE: THE BOY, WILL CODY

A SCENE FROM THE WILD WEST

8   "dancing sunshine": Wetmore, p. 1.

THE FORTUNE-TELLER MAKES A PREDICTION

9   "You will meet": Wetmore, p. 3.

9   "He was a superior being": Wetmore, p. 4.

9–10   "a mean horse" . . . "They all sayed": Goodman, p. 449.

10   "Your charge is to look after Willie": Goodman, p. 449.

11   "[I] took him outdoors": Goodman, p. 449.

SKINNY-DIPPING, SKIFFS, AND SKIPPING SCHOOL

11   "that exciting climate": Cody, *Life and Adventures*, p. 16.

11   "Why, I never knew": Cody, *An Autobiography*, p. 4.

11   "I was quite as bad": Cody, *Life and Adventures*, p. 17.

11   "By diligence": Cody, *Life and Adventures*, pp. 16–17.

12   "occupied so much": Cody, *Life and Adventures*, p. 17.

12 "We lost our presence of mind" . . . "We had stolen": Cody, *Life Story*, p. 20.

12–13 "I guess it" . . . "Aw, Ma": Thomas, p. 497.

13 "I greatly enjoyed": Cody, *Life Story*, p. 19.

A DARK AND MOURNFUL DAY

14 "Ah, Betsy Baker": Wetmore, p. 2.

15 "He died the next morning": Cody, *Life Story*, p. 20.

THE CODYS HEAD WEST

15 "Gloom fell over": Cody, *Life Story*, p. 20.

15 "Now is the time": McMaster, p. 215.

16 "at the best hotels": Goodman, p. 453.

16 "the most beautiful valley": Cody, *Life Story*, p. 26.

16 "got wild with excitement": Goodman, p. 455.

16 "Where [are] they going?" . . . "Utah and California": Cody, *Life Story*, p. 26.

16 "Oh, my": Goodman, p. 455.

16 "the first time I ever camped": Cody, *Life Story*, p. 29.

FLYING OVER THE PRAIRIE ON A PONY NAMED PRINCE

17 "conversations were very limited": Cody, *Life Story*, p. 28.

17 "I called him Prince": Cody, *Life Story*, p. 29.

17 "I was somewhat disappointed": Cody, *Life Story*, p. 28.

18 "genuine Western man" . . . "Oh, that's nothing": Cody, *Life Story*, pp. 30–34.

19 "Everything that he did": Cody, *Life Story*, p. 31.

19 "I had become": Cody, *Life Story*, p. 31.

BLEEDING KANSAS

19 "a hell of a storm": Eyal, p. 192.

19–20 "Kansas is the great battlefield": Lovejoy, p. 44.

20 "I can assure you": Lovejoy, p. 42.

20   "with the bayonet" . . . "to kill every damned abolitionist": pbs.org /wgbh/aia/part4/4p2952.html.

20   "Govern Kansas?": Nicholas, p. 139.

20   "We are in the midst": Pierson, p. 122.

A Speech and a Stabbing

21   "Speech! Speech!": Goodman, p. 459.

21–22   "Gentlemen, [Kansas] should be" . . . "I believe in letting": Cody, *Life and Adventures*, pp. 23–24.

23   "Mr. Cody, a noisy abolitionist": Gray, p. 5.

Death Threats, Disguises, and Danger

23   "brought upon our family": Cody, *Life and Adventures*, p. 25.

23   "My first real work": Cody, *An Autobiography*, p. 13.

24   "In less than one hour": Goodman, p. 460.

24   "It was a nice little school": Goodman, p. 464.

24   "damned abolitionist" . . . "As Cody [has] the most brats": Goodman, p. 464.

"The First Blood [Shed]"

25   "the first blood [shed]": Cody, *Life and Adventures*, p. 25.

Will versus Panthers and Neighbors

25   "You will have to be": Wetmore, p. 21.

25   "Willie drove the ponies": Goodman, p. 462.

26   "With the heart of a lion" . . . "rifle's sharp retort": Wetmore, pp. 15–16.

26   "We were almost daily": Cody, *Life Story*, p. 47.

27   "[I] thought Kansas was beautiful": Goodman, p. 468.

Father in the Shadows

28   "I've come to search the house" . . . "[This] is to cut": Wetmore, p. 23.

28   "Julia, you and Willie" . . . "We will be on the lookout": Goodman, pp. 465–66.

A TERROR-FILLED CHASE

29   "I'm going to warn Father": Goodman, p. 470.

29   "There's Cody's kid!": Cody, *An Autobiography*, p. 13.

29   "Let's go for him" . . . "Why, what is this?": Goodman, p. 470.

31   "dearer to me": Cody, *Life Story*, p. 46.

SAVING PRINCE

31   "They drove off all our stock": Cody, *An Autobiography*, p. 14.

31   "I was left": Goodman, p. 471.

31   "utter destitution" . . . "His presence, in fact": Cody, *An Autobiography*, p. 15.

32   "The loss of my faithful pony": Cody, *Life and Adventures*, p. 30.

32   "I came to get my pony" . . . "William F. Cody": Goodman, p. 474.

CHILDHOOD'S END

33   "As a result": Wetmore, p. 30.

33   "I made up my mind": Cody, *An Autobiography*, p. 15.

ACT TWO: BOY ON THE PLAINS

HARDSCRABBLE DAYS

36–37   "[We] planned what" . . . "I would do all the heavy work": Goodman, p. 476.

37   "wiry, little lad": Majors, p. 243.

37–38   "I can ride" . . . "No, sir, I will not": Goodman, pp. 476–77.

38   "big": Goodman, p. 477.

"DEAD IN LOVE"

39   "I, of course, could not go": Goodman, p. 479.

39   "The master of the school": Cody, *An Autobiography*, p. 25.

39–40   "blasted my prospects" . . . "I am killed": Cody, *Life and Adventures*, pp. 35–36.

40   "[Willie] Cody has murdered": Leonard and Goodman, p. 76.

40–41   "vengeance in his eye" . . . "kissing her and my sisters": Cody, *Life and Adventures*, pp. 37–38.

STAMPEDE!

41–42   "The wagons used in those days": Cody, *Life Story*, p. 66.

42–43   "About five hundred" . . . "Some of the wagons": Cody, *Life Story*, p. 73.

43   "enjoyable . . . no incidents": Cody, *Life Story*, p. 57.

43   "We have had many a laugh": Cody, *Life and Adventures*, p. 39.

MORMON WARS AND A STARVATION WINTER

44   "Everything ran along": Cody, *Life and Adventures*, p. 59.

44   "Woe, woe, to that man": Hafen and Hafen, p. 183.

44–45   "I intend to burn" . . . "On foot": Cody, *Life and Adventures*, p. 52.

45   "There was nothing to do": Cody, *An Autobiography*, p. 24.

45   "that we had to prop them up": Cody, *Life Story*, p. 78.

45   "I can honestly say": Cody, *Life Story*, p. 79.

PANNING FOR THE TRUTH

47   "Willie and I would": Goodman, p. 482.

47   "Say, that write up": William F. Cody to Julia Cody Goodman, June 11, 1911, in Foote, p. 72.

47   "A bright, keen-memoried": Gray, p. 14.

47   "He . . . impressed me": Russell, p. 35.

WILL GETS SCHOOLED

48   "My restless, roaming spirit": Cody, *Life Story*, p. 93.

48   "The wagon beds": Cody, *An Autobiography*, p. 30.

48   "I had nearly a thousand dollars": Cody, *An Autobiography*, p. 30.

48–49   "You couldn't even" . . . "At last, I really began": Cody, *An Autobiography*, p. 30.

49   "Will Cody" . . . "William Frederic[k] Cody": Majors, p. 245.

49   "plastered pretty well": Cody, *An Autobiography*, p. 34.

RIDING THE PONY EXPRESS

58   "My boy" . . . "I am the same boy": Cody, *Life Story*, p. 104.

58   "It was a long piece of road": Cody, *Life Story*, p. 104.

59   "all to pieces": Cody, *Life Story*, p. 91.

59   "My boy, you're a brick": Cody, *Life Story*, p. 105.

59   "A party of fifteen Indians" . . . "I told the people": Cody, *Life Story*, pp. 105–6.

60   "We knew full well" . . . "The recovered horses": Cody, *Life Story*, pp. 108–9.

PANNING FOR THE TRUTH

61   "can scarcely float": Gray, p. 19.

62   "I crossed the Plains": Lockwood, p. 28.

63   "was among the most noted": Majors, p. 176.

63   "There seems no point": Gray, p. 19.

63   "I'm inclined to think": McMurtry, p. 50.

GETTING EVEN

63   "The first rumblings": Cody, *An Autobiography*, p. 60.

64   "invading Missouri": Cody, *Life Story*, p. 126.

64   "[Jayhawkers] came upon us": Goodrich, p. 26.

64   "The tables are turned": Goodrich, p. 14.

64–65   "Having a longing": Cody, *Life Story*, p. 126.

WILL CODY: HORSE THIEF

65   "Secretly visit certain": Cody, *Life Story*, p. 127.

65   "This action may look like": Cody, *Life Story*, p. 127.

65   "It [is] neither": Cody, *Life Story*, p. 127.

66   "stealing themselves rich": Castel, p. 112.

66   "In Leavenworth we . . . 'ran things'": Cody, *Life Story*, p. 135.

66   "many a lively skirmish": Cody, *Life Story*, p. 134.

66   "They say you are" . . . "Perhaps these people": Cody, *Life Story*,
      p. 143.

67   "The [cash] that Willie brought home": Goodman, p. 489.

67   "What do you think" . . . "It did seem so nice": Goodman, pp. 489–90.

68   "I had money": Cody, *An Autobiography*, pp. 62–63.

68   "her flesh had been refined" . . . "only the names": Wetmore, pp. 105–7.

68   "She never complained": Cody, *An Autobiography*, p. 63.

68   "Thus passed away": Cody, *Life Story*, p. 135.

68   "United in death" . . . "I can't go home": Wetmore, p. 108.

68   "a very hard case" . . . "a dissolute and reckless life": Cody, *Life Story*,
      p. 135.

69   "after having been under the influence" . . . "I did not remember":
      Cody, *Life Story*, p. 135.

PRIVATE CODY

69   "a jolly good time": Cody, *Life Story*, p. 140.

ACT FOUR: BECOMING BUFFALO BILL

LULU

73–74 "William McDonald" . . . "In battle": Cody and Cooper, pp. 3–4.

74   "clean shaven . . . graceful": Cody and Cooper, p. 6.

74   "Her lovely face": Cody, *Life Story*, p. 141.

74   "I had been [educated]": Cody and Cooper, p. 29.

74   "I considered myself": Cody, *Life Story*, p. 141.

75   "an explorer's trip": Cody and Cooper, pp. 38–39.

75   "felt grieved": Cody, *Life Story*, p. 144.

75   "I began to realize": Cody and Cooper, p. 39.

75   "People generally said": Cody, *Life Story*, p. 145.

75–76 "What are we going to name it?" . . . "'Lo, Arta!": Cody and Cooper,
      p. 52.

"Looking Around for Anything"

76   "beer houses, whisky shops": Putnam, p. 198.

77   "[I was] railroading and trading": William F. Cody, Testimony in *Cody v. Cody*, WSA.

77   "In less than one month" . . . "the world by the tail": Cody, *Life Story*, p. 150.

78   "I dropped my arms aghast": Cody and Cooper, p. 65.

78   "You've got a flourishing little town" . . . "A ruinous stampede": Cody, *Life Story*, pp. 150–52.

79   "rather blue" . . . "I told her": William F. Cody, Testimony in *Cody v. Cody*, WSA.

"Buffalo Bill, Buffalo Bill, Never Missed and Never Will"

79   "was the fleetest steed": Cody, *Life Story*, p. 153.

79   "As soon as one" . . . "there were few men": Cody, *Life Story*, p. 155.

81   "During my engagement": Cody, *Life Story*, p. 162.

81   "Later, we pulled into camp": Cody, *Life Story*, p. 169.

81   "Here comes this old Bill" . . . "they connected the names": Cody, *True Tales*, p. 89.

82   "Buffalo Bill, Buffalo Bill": Russell, p. 90.

"Champion Buffalo Hunter of the Plains"

82   "Buffalo shooting match": Cody and Cooper, p. 122.

82–84   "A large crowd witnessed" . . . "Thereupon, the referees declared": Cody, *Life Story*, pp. 171–74.

84   "Of this [name]": Cody, *An Autobiography*, p. 118.

Panning for the Truth

84   "Persons from the east": Millbrook, p. 433.

85   "pretty well advertised": Cody, *Life Story*, p. 171.

85   "pick-up game": Yost, p. 17.

Stormy Days with Lulu

86   "She made little": William F. Cody, Testimony in *Cody v. Cody*, WSA.

86   "I didn't think": William F. Cody, Testimony in *Cody v. Cody*, WSA.

86   "At this time there was": Cody, *Life Story*, p. 175.

Galloping into a War Zone

87   "forever secure and guarantee": *House of Representatives for the Second Session of the Forty-Fourth Congress*, vol. 1, Washington: Government Printing Office, 1877, p. 68.

88   "Kill and scalp all": pbs.org/weta/thewest/program/episodes/four/whois.htm.

88   "We, of course, took": Hoig, p. 156.

89   "an Indian with a fat pony" . . . "If a village": historynet.com/hard-war-on-the-southern-plains.htm.

Bill Cody: Scout

90   "It was interesting": Cody, *Life Story*, p. 137.

91   "His eyesight is better": "The Wild West: Buffalo Bill and Dr. Carver Rocky Mountain and Prairie Exhibition," 1883 program, BBCW.

A Dangerous Undertaking

92   "I'll go": Cody, *Life Story*, p. 188.

92   "having no suitable place": Cody, *Life Story*, p. 175.

93   "I was afraid" . . . "General . . . I'll carry": Cody, *Life Story*, pp. 190–93.

93   "I gratefully accepted": Sheridan, vol. 2, pp. 300–01.

94   "We encountered hardships": Russell, p. 112.

A Tale of Tall Bull

96   "felt proud and elated": Cody, *Life Story*, p. 250.

96–97   "I was ordered" . . . "Little did I think": Cody, *Life Story*, pp. 255–60.

Panning for the Truth

98   "The wife begged": Paul, p. 55.

BUFFALO BILL, THE KING OF BORDER MEN

98   "Cody, allow me": Cody, *Life Story*, p. 263.

99   "During this short [ride]": Cody, *Life Story*, p. 264.

99   "wildest and truest story": Russell, p. 159.

99–100   "On through the mass": Kasson, p. 20.

PLAYING A JOKE ON MCCARTHY

101   "sports": Warren, p. 145.

101   "Should we dismount" . . . "I told the general": Cody, *Life Story*, pp. 290–91.

THE RETURN OF LULU

102   "a wonderful thing": Cody and Cooper, p. 161.

102–03   "far greater" . . . "I want him": Cody and Cooper, pp. 221–22.

PUTTING ON A LITTLE STYLE

103   "hunt buffalo, course the antelope": Davies, pp. 9–10.

103   "knobby and high-toned" . . . "I dressed in a new suit": Cody, *Life Story*, p. 282.

103   "As his horse came toward us": Davies, p. 29.

104   "For years afterward": Cody, *Famous Hunting Parties*, p. 137.

104   "buffalo tail [soup]": Cody, *Life Story*, p. 287.

BUFFALO BILL'S ROYAL PAIN

105   "I had but little": Cody, *Life Story*, p. 292.

105   "He is the most complete": Warren, p. 138.

105   "Antelope Jim": Warren, p. 138.

106   "[Custer] appeared": Warren, p. 148.

106   "He fired six shots": Cody, *Life Story*, p. 301.

ACT FIVE: STARRING BUFFALO BILL

A SCENE FROM THE WILD WEST

110   "Too late": Sell and Weybright, p. 156.

110   "I suppose they thought": Warren, p. 275.

111   "Whose was the right": "Buffalo Bill's Wild West and Congress of Rough Riders of the World," 1898 program, BBCW.

111   "The defeat of Custer": *Milwaukee Sentinel*, September 2, 1880.

SCOUTING IN TAILS AND A TOP HAT

112   "Everything [was] new": Cody, *Life Story*, p. 309.

112   "an imposing spectacle": Cody, *An Autobiography*, p. 247.

112   "more difficult for me": Cody, *Life Story*, p. 307.

112   "I was curious": Cody, *Life Story*, p. 310.

113   "Come out" . . . "I made a desperate effort": Cody, *Life Story*, p. 311.

113   "[You] might as well": Cody, *Life Story*, p. 311.

HONORS COME AND GO AND COME AGAIN

114   "Mr. William Cody's reputation": Russell, p. 187.

115   "nonetheless was deserving": nytimes.com/1989/07/09/us/buffalo-bill-s -medal-restored.html

BIG DECISIONS

115   "I made several": Cody, *Life Story*, p. 315.

115   "3 p.m. Mrs. Cody": Russell, p. 188.

116   "There is money in it": Cody, *Life Story*, p. 321.

116   "When my old 'pard'": Cody, *An Autobiography*, p. 257.

116   "I don't know just how bad": Cody and Cooper, p. 232.

116   "send [the children] to fine schools": Cody and Cooper, p. 231.

"HURRAH, HURRAH FOR *THE SCOUTS OF THE PRAIRIE*!"

116–17   "What the deuce" . . . "Come with me, boys": Cody, *Life Story*, p. 323.

117   "I never lay out": Monaghan, p. 250.

117–18   "Hurrah, hurrah": Monaghan, p. 252.

118   "I looked at my part" . . . "It'll take me": Cody, *Life Story*, p. 324.

STAGE FRIGHT BEFORE THE FOOTLIGHTS

118–19   "Where have you been" . . . "I chipped in": Cody, *Life Story*, pp. 326–27.

119   "not quite so good looking": Logan, p. 83.

119–20   "Oh, Mama, I am" . . . "Now you can understand": Cody and Cooper pp. 249–50.

120   "The only way" . . . "Paid!": Cody and Cooper, pp. 251–52.

120   "Texas Jack and myself": Cody, *Life Story*, p. 328.

SEASONS ONSTAGE

121   "a thrilling picture": Rosa and Mays, p. 53.

"A BEAUTIFUL ANGEL IN THAT BETTER WORLD"

122   "Good house, Papa": Wetmore, p. 227.

122   "he seemed to recognize me" . . . "But it was of no avail": Cody, *Life Story*, p. 339.

123   "God wanted him": William F. Cody to Julia Cody Goodman, April 22, 1876, in Foote, p. 13.

123   "to fight real Indians": Rosa and May, p. 55.

CUSTER'S LAST STAND

123   "absolute and undisturbed use": The Treaty of Fort Laramie, 1868, NARA.

123   "food pack": Utley, p. 126.

124   "The Sioux that [day]": smithsonianmag.com/history/how-the-battle -of-little-bighorn-was-won-63880188/?no-ist.

124   "Soldiers are coming!": Ward, p. 300.

124   "like hail on tepees": smithsonianmag.com/history/how-the-battle-of -little-bighorn-was-won-63880188/?no-ist.

124   "the battle lasted": pbs.org/weta/thewest/program/episodes/six/goodday.htm.

"THE FIRST SCALP FOR CUSTER"

125   "genuine battlefield martyr": Warren, p. 171.

126   "A running fight": Cody, *Life Story*, p. 343.

126–27   "a large party" . . . "It was no use": Cody, *Life Story*, pp. 343–44.

127   "I reeled slightly": Cody and Cooper, p. 269.

128   "The first scalp for Custer!": Cody, *Life Story*, p. 344.

PANNING FOR THE TRUTH

130   "From the manner": Russell, p. 226.

130   "The Indian . . . turned": Russell, p. 230.

"AIN'T THAT A NICE WAY FOR A WIFE TO ACT?"

132   "We had money" . . . "a house that was": Cody and Cooper, p. 278.

132   "My long and continued": Cody, *Life Story*, p. 363.

132   "I . . . attended to": Cody and Cooper, pp. 280–81.

132   "very much riled up": William F. Cody, Testimony in *Cody v. Cody*, WSA.

133   "Ain't that a nice way": William F. Cody to Julia Cody Goodman, March 9, 1882, in Foote, p. 18.

COWBOY FUN

134   "I had to call": Bratt, p. 279.

134   "There is nothing": Cody, *Life Story*, p. 363.

A "CRACKIN' GOOD" IDEA

135   "would encompass the whole" . . . "We mapped out": Salsbury, pp. 205–06.

135   "I did not feel": Salsbury, p. 206.

135–36   "would not smack" . . . "by the originals": Warren, p. 218.

136   "There will be an Indian fight": *Manchester Mirror and American* (NH), March 20, 1882.

136   "All those people back east": Cody and Cooper, p. 281.

147   "I have put up": William F. Cody to Julia Goodman Cody, September 24, 1883, in Foote, p. 21.

148   "If it was not for the hope": Fulton, pp. 159–60.

148   "Cody came to see me": Salsbury, p. 207.

148   "I solemnly promise": Russell, p. 303.

148–49 "chose in turn": Yost, p. 142.

SUNK, SOAKED, AND DISGUSTED

149   "Nearly one hundred": Cody, *Life and Adventures*, p. 312.

149   "Mounted on his": Sell and Weybright, p. 136.

150   "OUTFIT AT BOTTOM" . . . "GO TO NEW ORLEANS": Russell, p. 309.

150   "We opened on [time]": Cody, *Story of the Wild West*, p. 699.

150   "The camel's back": Walsh and Salsbury, pp. 242–43.

"THIS LITTLE MISSIE"

153   "I went right in": Russell, p. 313.

153   "This little missie": Russell, p. 313.

153   "A crowned queen": Sayers, p. 23.

153   "Her first shots": Fellows and Freeman, p. 73.

153   "quiet and ladylike manner": *Courier of London*, n.d., Annie Oakley Scrapbook, BBCW.

154   "What we want to do": Enss, *Buffalo Gals*, p. 107.

ONE SEASON WITH SITTING BULL

155   "Do you know who I am?": Ward, p. 351.

155–56 "establish a fictive" . . . "provide generously for": Jeffrey Means, e-mail communication to author, November 2, 2015.

156   "I am going to try hard": Kasson, p. 170.

156   "Please answer": William F. Cody to Lucius Q. C. Lamar, April 29, 1885, Records of the Commissioner of Indian Affairs, Letters Received, NARA.

156 "roving through the country": Moses, p. 69.

156 "Make a *very* emphatic *No*": Commissioner of Indian Affairs to William F. Cody, May 2, 1885, in Pfaller, p. 21.

158 "Merely riding": Kasson, p. 174.

158 "I am very glad": *Buffalo Daily Courier* (NY), June 13, 1885, Annie Oakley Scrapbook, BBCW.

159 "made a great pet of me": *Dramatic Review* (London), June 19, 1887, Annie Oakley Scrapbook, BBCW.

159 "kinship relationships" . . . "generous provider and protector": Jeffrey Means, e-mail communication to author, November 2, 2015.

159 "The Renowned Sioux Chief": Kasson, p. 177.

159 "speaks volumes": Kasson, p. 178.

159 "'friendship' offered": Kasson, p. 180.

160 "We take a great pleasure": McNenly, p. 58.

161 "The white man knows": Vestal, p. 251.

162 "indicated he did not": *St. Louis Critic*, October 3, 1885, Annie Oakley Scrapbook, BBCW.

162 "[He] is too grave": *St. Louis Critic*, October 3, 1885, Annie Oakley Scrapbook, BBCW.

163 "They treat me": *Buffalo Daily Courier* (NY), June 13, 1885, Annie Oakley Scrapbook, BBCW.

163 "[Did] he ever have any regret": Moses, p. 28.

163 "Tell this fool": Moses, p. 28.

163 "The wigwam is a better place": Moses, p. 30.

163–64 "My friend Long Hair": Vestal, p. 251.

SIGN-UP DAYS

164 "Cody selected the lucky individuals": Yost, p. 143.

165 "[He] is persistently": Yellow Robe, p. 225.

165 "heathenish ways": Moses, p. 69.

165 "cranks" . . . "exposing them to the superiority": William F. Cody to

Mike Russell, December 27, 1899, in Blackstone, *Business of Being*, p. 15.

PANNING FOR THE TRUTH

166   "courageous men and women": Warren, p. 359.

168   "I believe in immersing": Pratt, p. 335.

168   "Kill the Indian": Pratt, p. xi.

168   "will quickly fade": Warren, p. 363.

168   "began to resemble camps": McNenly, p. 65.

169   "Perhaps they realized": Moses, pp. 277–78.

169   "We were raised on horseback": http://segonku.unl.edu/~jheppler /showindian/analysis/progressive-image/bia-show.

171   "That is why" . . . "this is the way I get": Moses, p. 101.

WELCOME TO THE WILD WEST!

171   "America's National Entertainment": "Buffalo Bill's Wild West," 1887 program, BBCW.

172   "Cow-boy's Fun": "Buffalo Bill's Wild West," 1887 program, BBCW.

172   "[He is] the most imposing man": *Chicago Daily News*, May 5, 1893, Buffalo Bill Scrapbook, BBCW.

172   "There was enough firing": *New York Herald*, June 26, 1886, Nate Salsbury Scrapbook, DPL.

173   "Champion Boy Shot": Walsh, p. 253.

173   "men shooting from their saddles": Botkin, p. 142.

173   "Salute": "Buffalo Bill's Wild West," 1887 program, BBCW.

173–74   "There were no restrictions": Hawkeye, p. 160.

175–76   "could ride with a cup of water": Sell and Weybright, p. 151.

176   "Yankee pies": *New York Morning Journal*, July 5, 1888, Nate Salsbury Scrapbook, DPL.

176   "yelled and clapped": Foote, p. 24.

ACT SEVEN: ROUGH
RIDERS OF THE WORLD

A SCENE FROM THE WILD WEST

179   "The great interest": Remington, p. 96.

180   "graduates from [the] fierce school": "Buffalo Bill's Wild West and Congress of Rough Riders of the World," 1893 program, BBCW.

180   "grace of carriage": Burke, p. 43.

SEA-TOSSED SHOW

181   "sick as a cow": Cody, *Life and Adventures*, p. 318.

182   "a canvas city": Cody, *Life and Adventures*, p. 325.

182   "a storm of shouts": Yost, p. 187.

LASSOING LONDON

183   "was electric" . . . "Cody, you've fetched 'em": Cody, *Life and Adventures*, p. 329.

183   "apple pie order": Yost, p. 189.

183   "My old horse": Cody, *Life and Adventures*, p. 330.

184   "The Wild West is upon": *London Daily Chronicle*, May 6, 1887, Nate Salsbury Scrapbook, DPL.

184   "It is new": Cody, *Story of the Wild West*, p. 734.

184   "The crush and fight": *London Evening News and Telegraph*, May 19, 1887, Nate Salsbury Scrapbook, DPL.

185   "coal black eyes": Manchester, England, newspaper (title unknown), April 28, 1887, Johnny Baker Scrapbook, DPL.

185   "Everyone is of the opinion": *Court and Society Review*, April 27, 1887, Johnny Baker Scrapbook, DPL.

185   "It's pretty hard work": Warren, p. 324.

186   "A few years ago": Yost, p. 199.

"GRANDMOTHER ENGLAND"

186–87   "but never since": Warren, p. 320.

187   "Indians . . . cowboys, Mexicans": Rosa and Mays, p. 119.

187   "Grandmother England": Black Elk and Neihardt, p. 177.

A SAD EVENT AT SEA

188   "We are doing": *Brooklyn Daily Eagle*, January 22, 1888, Buffalo Bill Scrapbook, BBCW.

188   "He seemed to be" . . . "We could almost": Cody, *Life and Adventures*, p. 337.

"HERO OF TWO CONTINENTS"

189   "Hero of Two Continents": Cody, *Story of the Wild West*, pp. 764–65.

190   "Nothing very original": Warren, p. 296.

190   "The presence of the Queen": Wetmore, p. 276.

190   "best known man": *Lincoln County Tribune*, June 23, 1888, Johnny Baker Scrapbook, DPL.

190   "The man of the year": Russell, p. 341.

HARD LIVING WITH LULU

191   "I would give anything": Warren, p. 345.

192   "My wife and I": William F. Cody to Mollie Moses, April 17, 1885, BBCW.

192   "Go to the St. James Hotel": William F. Cody to Mollie Moses, April 26, 1886, BBCW.

192   "the finest looking woman": Rosa and May, p. 160.

193   "If only Lulu": William F. Cody to Al Goodman, July 12, 1888, BBCW.

193   "Send the bill": Yost, p. 247.

194   "Are you awake?" . . . "Willie, it will soon": Warren, p. 347.

TRIUMPH IN PARIS

195   "the Napoleon of the prairie": *New York Home Journal*, July 12, 1899, Buffalo Bill Scrapbook, BBCW.

195   "[The performers] are already": *New York Times*, May 19, 1889, p. 1.

195   "I shot a bullet": *Chicago Tribune*, January 13, 1888, p. 6.

196   "Observing [the people]": Klumpke, p. 193.

TRAGEDY ON TOUR

198   "He seemed genuinely moved": Burke, p. 244.

198   "Such gaudy warriors": Moses, p. 88.

SUSPICIONS, ALLEGATIONS, AND INVESTIGATIONS

198   "The more I see": *New York Herald* (Paris edition), March 16, 1890, Buffalo Bill Scrapbook, BBCW.

198–99   "conform to the white": Moses, p. 74.

200   "notoriety-seeking busybodies": Walsh and Salsbury, p. 280.

200–01   "If [the show] did not suit me" . . . "That is not to be listened to": "Examination of the Indians Traveling with Cody and Salsbury's Wild West Show by Acting Commissioner of Indian Affairs," in Robert V. Belt to Secretary of the Interior, November 18, 1890, Records of the CIA Correspondence Land Division, NARA.

GHOST DANCE

202   "would bring with him": Russell, p. 355.

202   "help your [Indian] agents": Louis S. Warren, correspondence with author, February 14, 2014.

202   "make ready to join": McLaughlin, p. 185.

203   "I was sure": Cody, *True Tales*, p. 235.

MASSACRE

204   "Those . . . stupid Indian agents": Yost, p. 468.

204   "I can still see": Black Elk and Neihardt, p. 218.

205   "For six weeks": Moses, p. 111.

WILD WEST, HO!

206 "The main elements": Blackstone, *Buckskin, Bullets and Business*, p. 107.

ACT EIGHT: SHOW'S END

LIFE WITHOUT BILL

210 "wilder than a goldurned coyote": Yost, p. 283.

211 "all joy and happiness": Yost, p. 307.

211 "I thought I would paint": William F. Cody to Al Goodman, August 25, 1891, in Foote, p. 38.

211–12 "I have lost": Walsh and Salsbury, p. 237.

A TOWN CALLED CODY

212 "perfect homes" . . . "verdant mountain valley": Warren, p. 474.

212 "stinking water": Warren, p. 476.

212 "I have to brave it": Warren, p. 487.

213–14 "I want to be known": Walsh and Salsbury, p. 327.

214 "He always had words" . . . "How [are you] getting along?": Warren, p. 488.

215 "That dear old country": Blackstone, *Business of Being*, p. 28.

CODY V. CODY

215 "God did not intend": William F. Cody to Julia Cody Goodman, March 21, 1902, in Foote, p. 49.

215 "Then it's war and publicity": William F. Cody to Julia Cody Goodman, March 21, 1902, in Foote, p. 49.

215 "We're Liable": Yost, p. 323.

215 "I think I am entitled": William F. Cody to Julia Cody Goodman, July 1903, in Foote, p. 57.

216 "It's your fault!": Warren, p. 503.

216 "Do you still love" . . . "Yes I do": Enss, *Many Loves*, pp. 94–95.

Saying Goodbye Again and Again and Again

217   "Say, isn't it glorious": William F. Cody to Julia Cody Goodman, March 17, 1903, in Foote, p. 53.

217   "I'll stick right": Blackstone, *Business of Being*, p. 43.

218   "When I went away": Russell, p. 450.

218   "There was not a dry eye": Russell, p. 451.

218   "Just one more": Russell, p. 450.

A Couple Once More

219   "forgiven for the past" . . . "willing, but some things": Yost, p. 364.

220   "We've had peaceful": *North Platte Telegraph*, April 14, 1910, Buffalo Bill Scrapbook, BBCW.

220   "I have forgotten": "Posthumous Memoirs of Colonel William F. Cody," Unidentified Clip File, BBCW.

Busted!

221   "I am not down and out": Yost, p. 386.

The Story of Isham

221–22   "Are you going to the sale?" . . . "[Bill] broke down": Yost, p. 387.

End of the Trail

222   "I am very tired": William F. Cody to Julia Cody Goodman, August 22, 1915, in Foote, p. 76.

The Last Ride

223   "I've still got my boots on": Cody and Cooper, p. 321.

224   "Soon [I] will go": Sell and Weybright, p. 255.

224   "frail, white-faced" . . . "The doctor says": Cody and Cooper, p. 322.

224   "We played a game": Boal, n.p.

224   "He would imagine": Warren, p. 549.

224   "The old scout": Thomas, p. 495.

224   "I wish Johnny": Cody and Cooper, p. 324.

226   "the greatest plainsman": Yost, p. 400.

226   "The Oglala Sioux": Blackstone, *Business of Being*, p. 84.

226   "It's pretty up there": Cody and Cooper, p. 325.

227   "Let my show go on": Russell, p. 481.

PICTURE CREDITS

Many thanks to the organizations and people cited for their generous contributions.

Buffalo Bill Center of the West: x, 2, 9, 10, 69, 70, 102, 107, 128, 187

Buffalo Bill Museum and Grave, Lookout Mountain, Golden, Colorado: 41, 73, 115, 122, 131, 143, 172, 174, 189, 194, 211, 213, 214, 217, 219, 225

W. C. Farmer: 52

Candace Fleming/Author Collection: 22, 30, 78, 80, 125, 196

The Denver Public Library, Western History Collection [Call # NS-23]: 184

The Denver Public Library, Western History Collection [Call # NS-271]: 34

The Denver Public Library, Western History Collection [Call # NS-296]: 152

The Denver Public Library, Western History Collection [Call # NS-479]: 178

The Denver Public Library, Western History Collection [Call # NS-591]: 108

The Denver Public Library, Western History Collection [Call # NS-687]: 173

The Denver Public Library, Western History Collection [Call # X-33465]: 6

The Denver Public Library, Western History Collection [Call # X-33472]: 208

Library of Congress: 55, 76, 91, 111, 117, 140, 146, 160, 161, 164, 165, 167, 169, 170, 175, 181, 205, 228

Eric Rohmann: 134

INDEX

railroad construction in, 76–79, 76, 86

See also Leavenworth

Kansas Pacific Railroad, 76, 80–82

Kerngood, Moses, 127, 128

Kickapoo Indians, 17

Kills Plenty, 198

Kiowa Indians, 90–92

Lakota Sioux, 113–14, 167–68, 180, 185

deaths during European tour of, 198

in Wild West show, 4, 6, 7–8, *34*, 35–36, 71, 110, 154–56, 159, 164, 170, 172, 183, 205, 209

Wounded Knee massacre of, 204

Lamar, Lucius, 156–57

Lame White Man, Chief, 124

Leavenworth (Kansas), 37–38, 48, 56, 66, 68, 74

See also Fort Leavenworth

Le Claire (Iowa), 9, 11, 13

Leo XIII, Pope, 197–98

Lillie, Gordon William "Pawnee Bill," 218, 220

Lincoln (Nebraska), 194

Little Ring, 197

London (England), 3–5, 181–88, 191

London Daily Chronicle, 184

London Evening News, 184

Longfellow, Henry Wadsworth, 110–11

Louise, Princess, 183

Louisville (Kentucky), 151

Lovejoy, Julia, 20

Madsen, Chris, 130

Majors, Alexander, 37, 38, 48, 63

Manchester (England), 188

Maud, Princess, 183

McDonald, Orra, 115

McDonald, William, 72–73, *73*

McGee, George, 61

McLaughlin, James, 155, 202–203

McPherson Station, 100, 113

Means, Jeffrey, 155–56

Medal of Honor, 114–15

Merritt, Colonel Wesley, 126–27

Mexican vaqueros, 4, 137, 171, 173, 182, 187

Milan (Italy), 197

Miles, General Nelson, 201, 202, 204–205

Miller, "Broncho Charlie," 4

Miller, Charles, 59, 61

Miller Brothers and Arlington 101 Ranch Wild West, 222

Milligan, W. F., 118–19

Mills, Colonel Anson, 123

Miniconjou Indians, 113–14

Mississippi, 69

Missouri, 16, 21, 69, 147

Jayhawkers and Red Legs attacks in, 64–66

pro-slavery ruffians in Kansas from, 20, 25, 32

Montana, 213

Montreal (Canada), 159

Moore, Major Alick, 115

Morgan, Thomas Jefferson, 198–99

Mormons, 44–46

Mormon Trail, 57

Moses, Mollie, 192